Gribby
The most ~~~~ group... of course. Enjoy your trip and cherish all of the laughs & such. The last four

The Bad Girl's Guide to the Open Road

years have flown by!! Good luck where ever your road takes you!!
Be Safe!
☺ Hendey

*Book has ↓ Securely been edited for an age appropriate trip!!
☺

The *Bad Girl's*

CHRONICLE BOOKS
SAN FRANCISCO

Guide to the Open Road

by Cameron Tuttle

Illustrations by
Susannah Bettag

Text copyright © 1999 by Cameron Tuttle

Illustrations copyright © 1999 by Susannah Bettag

Library of Congress Cataloging-in-Publication Data:
Tuttle, Cameron.
   The bad girl's guide to the open road / by Cameron Tuttle ;
   illustrations by Susannah Bettag.
         p.   cm.
   ISBN 0-8118-2170-6
   1. Automobile touring. 2. Women automobile drivers. I. Title.
GV1023.T78   1999
796.7'082—dc21   98-39634
                                  CIP

Printed in the United States of America.

Designed by Pamela Geismar

Distributed in Canada by Raincoast Books
9050 Shaughnessy Street
Vancouver, British Columbia V6P 6E5

20 19 18 17 16 15 14 13 12 11

Chronicle Books LLC
85 Second Street
San Francisco, California 94105

www.chroniclebooks.com

Acknowledgments

I would like to thank Susan Blinkhorn for her inspiration and bad girl sense of humor; Dorothea Herrey for her belief in this project from the start; Dana Horstmann for her research expertise and tireless efforts to keep me sane during the writing process; my agent, Charlotte Sheedy, for her enthusiasm, guidance, and vision; my editor, Kate Chynoweth, for her innate sense of the art of badness and for taking the book so much to heart that she left on an endless road trip and hasn't been heard from again; my technical advisors, Laura Rauch and Raymond Long; and Halle Becker, who is and always will be the ultimate bad girl.

And special thanks to my friends and family who listened to me talk about this project for years, all smiling politely while pretending to understand what the hell I was talking about.

at the gym. It's time to hit the road when you secretly record talk shows for your

Bad Girl's Menu

Quiz of the Day

"Are You a Road Sister?" 24

*A Daily Requirement for putting
together a bad-ass traveling squad*

Start Your Engine 11

*All starters come with a bad attitude and your choice of
appetizing reasons to hit the road.*

On the Side . . .

On the Road 48

*All entries are served hot off the grille and seasoned
with spicy beauty tips for bad girls. Get it to go!*

more goodies on the back

Off the Road 115

All entries are 98 percent fact-free, drizzled with local color and served with light roadside dishes.

The End of the Road 164

All entries are peppered with humor and served raw with your choice of free-range bad girl pranks.

save room for our . . .

Destination Directory 178

introduction

Despite what you've seen in the movies, you don't have to kill a man to go on a road trip. Just wanting to kill someone is enough. If you're feeling overwhelmed, depressed, crazy, bored, exhausted, or all of the above, then it's time to hit the road.

Road tripping is you in a car with an open throttle and an open mind. It's the ultimate brain douche that clears your head and leaves you feeling fresh. It's freedom in fast-forward, a movable feast, and a ticket to ride. Road tripping gives you the chance to recreate yourself at every stop, break the rules, and escape the trappings of your dreary, everyday existence. And it's an open invitation to be bad—whatever that means to you—cop a bad attitude, use bad judgment, have a bad hair day, all week long.

The Bad Girl's Guide to the Open Road is filled with the best and the worst of my road trip experiences. It has everything a woman needs to know about low-budget, high-adventure, safe road tripping. It's the ultimate read-it-before-you-leave, throw-it-in-the-glove-compartment, use-it-if-you-run-out-of-toilet-paper handbook for any woman searching for the key to fulfillment and lasting happiness—the road trip.

You go, girl! Your life is an open road.

Start Your Engine

1

*R*emember those family vacations from your childhood, when you spent day after endless day trapped in the back of a sweltering station wagon stuck to the hot vinyl seats with nothing but a Styrofoam ice chest between you and your whining, pinching, biting, carsick siblings while your mother read from some boring guidebook and your father drove frantically from one **landmock** to the next? That was not road tripping.

landmock n a pseudohistorical site given "landmark" status in order to make money off of overpriced admission fees and souvenirs

Road tripping is an auto-erotic adventure where you get to do the things you don't allow yourself to do at home. Eat like a pig. Wear the same underwear for days. Chew tobacco. Flirt with strangers. Have beef jerky for breakfast. Go-go dance in a wet tube top. Get up to watch the sun rise or sleep until noon. Whatever sounds good, the road is the place to do it.

A road trip can be anything you want it to be. You decide how to act, where to go, when to stop, and what to do when you stop. You can take chances (drive bottomless through the "Show Me State"), express yourself (sing "Respect" in the VIP Lounge at the Ramada Inn in Topeka), drive under the influence of an assumed identity (Thelma, Louise, Towanda), or just be yourself. No

fresh air. **It's time to hit the road when you're afraid to leave the house without**

one knows you on the road and no one expects a damn thing from you.

To the untrained eye, road tripping looks like plain old car travel—it's not. Car travel is work. You know where you're going, why you're going there, and you're probably trying to get there as fast as possible. It's something you endure rather than enjoy. Car travel requires no stretch of the imagination, no mental adjustment, no risk taking, and no attitude. All that matters is hauling your ass from point A to point B.

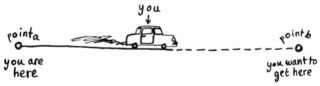

Road tripping is much more than a way of travel—it's a way of life. It's all the unique, peak, and freak experiences you have along the way. It's the people you hustle when shooting pool in a **cross your heart bar** miles from any interstate, the tell-all conversations you have with total strangers you're hoping will buy you another beer, and the food you eat in towns so small that the calories don't even count.

cross your heart bar n *any down and dirty roadside bar that looks too bad to pass up but kinda makes you want to cross your heart for luck before you step inside*

Road tripping is exploring back roads, cruising through the cracks and crevices of an America you can't read

wearing makeup. **It's time to hit the road when you have no idea what to do when**

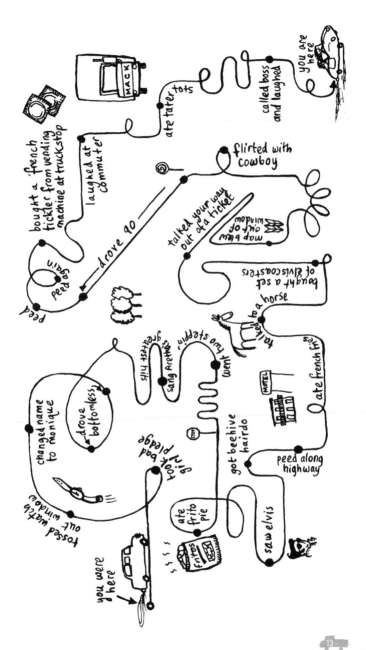

you're not at work.   It's time to hit the road when you actually believe that

about in any book. It's a personal pilgrimage to the road-side altars of Americana and a chance to worship this country's crazy cultural delights and natural treasures. Trading posts. Plastic lawn decorations. Chain-saw sculptures. Rodeos. Spam sandwiches. Mailbox art. Drive-thru liquor stores and drive-in wedding chapels. Monuments carved out of granite and testaments of love carved in Formica.

What should you expect to happen on a road trip? Expect nothing. Every road trip is unique because it's real life in real time. And every road trip *should* be different. If you try to control the experience, you're not road tripping, you're power tripping. And that means you're missing the whole point.

One of the best things about road tripping is that you don't know what's around the bend. In a world in which we're taught to feel like underachievers if we aren't constantly overscheduled, the simple act of not knowing can set you free.

Your first day on the road, something strange and magical happens. You feel happy. As you think about your life and all of the things that were making you crazy, nothing seems so bad. In fact, it's all pretty funny.

Want to see how bad you look but can't find a full-length mirror? Just pull up behind one of those shiny stainless-steel tanker trucks at a gas station or truck stop. If you stand behind the truck, you can see your full-length reflection in the tank's butt. It's a little like a fun-house mirror—but it works.

fashion matters. It's time to hit the road when all of your best friends have

Suddenly, you're free—you've got **rearview-mirror perspective**.

rearview-mirror perspective n *a mood-altering shift in perspective when you realize that* problems in your life are smaller than they appear

By the second day your brain gets all loose and tingly. It can't be explained scientifically, but it looks something like this:

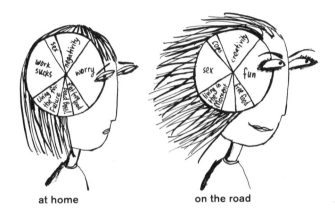

at home   **on the road**

You may even have a fuel-injected awakening that hits you like a bug going 70 and you realize that you don't have time to wait for a knight in shining armor to carry you away from your troubles—a Mustang and a can of Armor All will do just fine. You'll scratch bikini wax off your to-do list and replace it with Turtle Wax. You'll forget about your promise to hit the gym every day when you hit the open road and feel the wind on your face and the sweat on the backs of your thighs—no matter how wide.

After only a few days of freedom, nearly everything about you will change. You'll act differently, look different, and smell different too.

A Typical Road Tripper's Transformation

	TRAVEL LOG—DAY **ONE**	TRAVEL LOG—DAY **THREE**	TRAVEL LOG—DAY **FIVE**
Departure Time:	7:50 A.M.	Sometime before noon	Time is an illusion. Besides, I like it here.
Breakfast:	Coffee with skim milk and Equal Grapefruit half Bagel with lowfat cream cheese	Coffee with milk and sugar Chocolate-covered donut with sprinkles Beef jerky for the road	Tall glass of Coca-Cola, no ice Eggs, bacon, grits, buttermilk biscuits Side of fries and a bowl of stewed prunes
Itinerary:	Coffee break at 10:30 A.M. Lunch after 250 miles Call to confirm motel reservation before 5:00 P.M.	Head west, sort of Stop for gas before hitting the reserve tank	Is it Wednesday or Thursday?
Appearance:	Hair pulled back in a neat ponytail Light eye makeup with just a hint of lip-stick Clean denim shirt tucked into freshly pressed khaki shorts White tennis socks and canvas sneakers	Hair down and windblown, no makeup Slight sunburn on left arm Hairy nubs on unshaven legs Shirt untucked, sleeves rolled up, chili stains on wrinkled shorts Shoes, no socks	Ripped the sleeves off the denim shirt and tied one around my head—it just feels right Hair stays back and out of my eyes better when I only wash it once a week Driving barefoot gives me better control (traded my shoes for a glow-in-the-dark compass, a Zippo lighter, and a six-pack of Rolling Rock) Wow, I'm really tan—or dirty

Attitude:	Should I really be doing this? Where will this get me in life?	What's one more day? They probably haven't even noticed that I'm gone. My life can wait.	Maybe I won't go back to my life. What's the worst thing that can happen? Hey, this *is* my life.
Worries:	I think I left the coffee maker on. If I miss *Ally McBeal*, all my friends will be making references to an episode I haven't seen, compounding my fears that they're always doing really fun stuff without me.	I hope they'll take payment in the form of a stand-up routine at happy hour tonight. Will I be able to pick up a classic rock station driving through the Bible Belt?	I hope Tumbleweed Junction has blueberry pancakes instead of banana tomorrow. That was just a cold sore on his lip, right?
Sex Life:	So it's been a year. I have more important things to do with my time.	So *that's* what all the hoopla's about.	Is Trojan a publicly held company?
Career Outlook:	Maybe I should go to law school.	Maybe I'll join the forest service.	I think there's a certain art to flipping burgers
Religious Outlook:	Lord help me.	God Bless America!	I must have been a '66 Mustang in a former life.
Today's Highlights:	Read every historical marker on Route 1 Found super unleaded for under $1.25 a gallon No tickets, no accidents	Watched a bull being castrated Learned to two-step at Studs 'n' Suds Bought massive quantities of illegal fireworks, then shot a bottle rocket at a rude trucker	Killer game of "What's that cloud look like?" on Highway 151 Bubba's BBQ in Kingston, Mississippi Picked up the cutest hitchhiker—and I do mean *picked up*

Think of road tripping as an anxiety exfoliater. With every new experience, you'll shed layers of old, dead worries—revealing the brighter, more vibrant and carefree you underneath. Of course, you'll still find things to worry about on the road, it's human nature. But the anxiety you feel when road tripping is a refreshing charge of adrenaline compared to homegrown stress.

Anxiety Is Relative

Questions you ask yourself . . .

AT HOME	ON THE ROAD
How will I possibly pay this bill?	Did he say his name was Bill?
Does my health insurance cover therapy?	Is the toilet seat covered with pee?
Have I made a terrible career choice that will lead to nothing but a life of unhappiness?	Left or right at the light?
Should I go back to school and get another degree?	Should I go back and get another plate of ribs?
Why are nice guys such a turnoff?	Did I miss the turnoff?
Is it possible to freeze a few eggs in case I don't meet Mr. Right until I'm in my forties?	Scrambled or fried?
Is my cholesterol too high?	Should I pull over and get high?

road when you hate your job so much that you go to the bathroom just to pass the

Q: How can you visit Brazil, Denmark, Paris, Rome, Milan, Belfast, and Moscow without a passport?

A: Road trip through Tennessee

Once you start talking about going on a road trip, you'll probably take some heat from other people. Most people don't want to you to get away and be happy—they want you to stay with them and suffer. But don't ignore the losers who tell you that road tripping is a frivolous escape. Just say, "You got that right. See ya!"

Then get in your car and drive for your life.

As you head on down the road, you'll see a brown cow, pass a greasy diner, and study a cluster of clouds in the sky. Soon you can't help asking yourself deep questions about life: Do cows fall in love? Where does traffic start? What do clouds smell like? Why doesn't Demi Moore have stretch marks? Do greasy diners attract people with big hair or make hair bigger? Is that guy in the rusted-out Chevy truck waving at me?

Suddenly, you're feeling fast and sassy. You crank the tunes, lean hard on the pedal, catch up to the guy in the Chevy, and wave him down. You introduce yourself as Roxanne El Dorado—Roxy to your friends. He buys you a cold beer at a roadside cantina. If you like him, you buy him a beer. If you don't, you climb out the window of the ladies room, jump into your car, and burn rubber out of the parking lot, spraying gravel and attitude. *Hasta la vista,* dude!

the traveling squad

The girls you go with are as important as where you go. You can always just hit the road with your best friend and have a gas. But you may want to travel with someone you don't already know every little thing about, someone who will surprise you along the way. Be smart and choose **road sisters** who bring something special to the party. If you're broke, invite a chick with a trust fund or at least more credit than you have—kidnap her if you have to. If your antenna snapped off and static is music to your ears, bring someone with a killer collection of tunes. If your car just got the boot, find anyone with a car or, better yet, a convertible.

road sister n *1: a woman who road trips with style, especially one who has road tripped with you, a fellow bad girl, a* **Gohemian** *girl, one of your roadies 2: someone with no shame, no fear, and no scruples about bending the law when necessary*

Gohemian *n one who lives an unconventional life on the go;* adj *nomadic;* v *to go wild ("She just couldn't go back to her old ways, so she went* gohemian.*")*

Putting a traveling squad together is like casting a sit-com. The more variety you bring on board, the better

Q: What car did Thelma and Louise drive?
A: 1966 Thunderbird convertible

turned to powder. It's time to hit the road when someone gives you a copy of

your chances of a long and entertaining ride. Think of yourself as the star and select a supporting cast that includes a sister who makes you laugh, a sister who makes you look good, and a sister who challenges your thinking on every little thing. Be sure that any prospective road sister is someone you really want to know like a sister. On the road, **bad girl bondage** is unavoidable and it sticks for life.

bad girl bondage n *1: a state of being connected on the spiritual plane of badness 2: high-octane, high-speed, high-caloric female bonding that typically occurs on the road*

When you start to notice a buildup of road grime on your face, it's time for an invigorating, exfoliating facial scrub. You can pick up the necessary ingredients at any coffee shop or fast-food joint for free.

What you need: two packets of sugar and one packet of honey.

What to do: Rinse your face with warm water. Empty the sugar packets into the palm of one hand and drizzle with honey. Mix with a finger until it has the consistency of a grainy paste. Then apply a thin layer to your face, add a little warm water as you go, and massage vigorously. Rinse with warm water and pat dry.

This sweet scrub stimulates circulation, sloughs off dead skin—and it's finger-lickin' good. Follow this with a mayonnaise moisturizing mask. Spread a thin layer of mayo all over your face, leave it on for 10 to 15 minutes, then rinse with warm water.

Traveling in threes on a road trip has definite advantages. You always have someone to create a diversion, someone to gang up on, and someone to break a tie—and you still have room in the car for a hunky hitchhiker. When you do a three-for-the-road trip, have a contrarian along for bonus laughs. If two of you are Democrats, bring a Republican for heated debates and added protection through the Bible Belt. If two of you are real road warriors, bring along a "road worrier," someone who can be the designated driver at night or bail you out of jail in the morning.

Q: In 1997, which U.S. state legalized eating your own roadkill?
A: West Virginia

The Rules. It's time to hit the road when the checkout line you're waiting in

There's no shame in road tripping alone. Some of the most intense spiritual awakenings and kick-ass adventures happen when you're flying solo. You've got time to think in the car and time to talk in the bar. There's something spiritual about swapping stories, secrets, or spit with a perfect stranger, someone you know you'll never see again.

Before you hit the road with anyone other than your dog, take this quiz to see if you and your potential traveling companions will be road sisters or **roadkill**. If a cool friend at home turns into a **B.O.W.** after a few days of roughing it, you'll be a **P.O.W.**

roadkill n *1: a bummer, a downer, a buzzkill 2: dead, often flattened animals found on or beside the road 3: dinner in some Southern states*

B.O.W. n *1: Bitch on Wheels or Brat on Wheels 2: someone who doesn't travel well and can't handle the free-form on-the-road existence*

P.O.W. n *1: Prisoner on Wheels 2: how you feel when trapped on a road trip with a B.O.W. or an **airbag***

airbag n *passenger who has nothing to say and won't shut up*

closes and you burst into tears. It's time to hit the road when you cackle through

Are You a Road Sister?

1. A passing lane is for ____?
A. passing cars
B. making passes
C. passing gas

2. Ideally, my road-trip budget is ____.
A. 25 dollars a day
B. 50 dollars a day
C. completely irrelevant until my credit cards are maxed out

3. On a typical day, I pee ____.
A. two to three times a day
B. two to three times an hour
C. in my pants when I laugh really hard

4. A V-8 is ____.
A. the perfect low-cal meal
B. an internal combustion engine with eight cylinders
C. a cheerleading routine popular in the South

5. The best reason to road trip is ____.
A. I can't afford to fly
B. my mental health
C. roadkill jerky

6. "Slippery When Wet" signs make me ____.
A. slow down and proceed with caution
B. think about baby seals
C. really horny

7. When I see a cute hitchhiker, I usually ____.
A. mouth "sorry" as I drive past
B. slow down, check him out, then smile and floor it
C. slow down, check him out, hit him gently with the car, then tie him to the roof with duct tape to play with later

8. I'd rather ____ than change a tire myself.
A. call AAA
B. flag down someone who can help
C. sell the car

9. If I were a roadside sign, I'd be ____.
A. Slow Children Playing
B. Dangerous Curves
C. Wildlife Ahead

10. Peeing beside the car is:
A. disgusting and a crime
B. better than peeing inside the car
C. a religious experience

11. I brake for ____.
A. coffee and cheap unleaded gas
B. roadside folk art
C. Elvis and all of the above

[A Quiz]

12. Speed limit signs are:
A. to be honored under all circumstances
B. unrealistic guides to help motorists drive safely
C. perfect for target practice

13. I believe that _____.
A. schedules are absolutely necessary and should always be followed
B. schedules and road trips don't mix
C. schedules and those who try to impose them should be thrown from the car at high speeds

14. Sticky buns are _____.
A. sinful cinnamon rolls to be eaten only once a year—and only if I work out afterward
B. a light snack
C. what happens when you don't shower for a few days

15. I am happiest when I eat:
A. two or three meals a day
B. two or three plates of barbecue at one sitting
C. two or three plates of barbecue two or three times a day

16. When I see a bug hit the windshield, I think _____.
A. that's really sad; I can feel its pain
B. that's what windshield wipers are for, right?
C. the colors are amazing, especially the yellow ones

17. When I hit the road, I always pack _____.
A. moist towelettes
B. a squirt gun
C. chewing tobacco in my right cheek

If you answered **A** to most questions, you are a sister road worrier. Compassionate and responsible, you always play by the rules—if you play at all. You'll have to ride in the backseat until you loosen up.

If you answered **B** to most questions, you are a sister go-girl. Pragmatic and car smart, you like to go with the flow and have fun. You can ride shotgun anytime.

If you answered **C** to most questions, you are a sister bad supreme. Fast and fearless, you are the ultimate bad girl and an inspiration to all road sisters. You won't be happy unless you're behind the wheel, steering with your feet.

what to bring

In a perfect world, the ultimate road trip requires no planning and no packing. It's pleasure in its purest form, like swimming without a suit, TV without commercials, sex without a condom. It happens spontaneously. You're heading to 7-Eleven for a six-pack on a warm, barefoot evening, when suddenly you hear the call of **Mother Road** and just keep on driving.

Mother Road n *the mythical goddess of the road who has the power to guide, instruct, and empower; she's a lot like Mother Nature—you don't want to piss her off ("I couldn't find it on the map so I asked* Mother Road *whether I should turn left or right. She told me to pull off the road, have a few shots of tequila, and let it come to me.")*

Unfortunately, we don't live in a perfect world. So here are a few quick things to think about before you squeal out of the driveway and off into the sunset.

The Bare Essentials

A road trip is about leaving it all behind—physically and mentally. You can't escape the trappings of your life if you haul it all with you. And you can't expect much of an adventure if you're not willing to rough it a bit. So strip down to the bare essentials and push the limits of your comfort zone. Letting go of all the material crap you think you need is a freeing experience.

Of course, the definition of essential varies from trip-per to tripper, and there may be times when you feel the need to indulge in a frivolous item or two. Just be sure of three things: 1. you have room for the occasional hitch-hiker; 2. you can see out the rear window; 3. your emotional ties to your possessions are loose enough to withstand watching them blow out the window.

A Car:

There's no way around it, you need a car—ideally, one that runs faster than you do. But anything that moves forward will do. The car should have a working engine, four tires, and enough gas in the tank to put some distance between you and what's making you crazy. It doesn't have to be new, sexy, or fast, but it has to have soul, a stereo, and a name. Every getaway car deserves a name with character—the Badmobile, the Hog, Big Brother, the Whale, Eloise, or whatever.

Road Tunes:

If you plan ahead for only one part of your trip, make it the road tunes. The songs you play along the way set the tone for the whole trip. They will be your constant companions, your mood-altering drugs, and, best of all, the sound track to your adventure. Choose the kind of music that gets your motor running and go for a wide variety. I don't know if this works for weddings, but it's a tried-and-true rule for road tunes: Take something old, something new, something borrowed, and something blue, and you'll be happy. And be sure to take about twice as many tapes or CDs as you think you'll need.

Recommended

All I Wanna Do Is Have Some Fun *(Sheryl Crow)*

Leaving Las Vegas *(Sheryl Crow)*

Criminal *(Fiona Apple)*

On & On *(Erykah Badu)*

Looking Forward *(Mary Black)*

Hand in My Pocket *(Alanis Morissette)*

One Way Ticket *(LeAnn Rimes)*

Who's Zoomin' Who *(Aretha Franklin)*

Respect *(Aretha Franklin)*

Think *(Aretha Franklin)*

Sisters Are Doing It for Themselves

(Aretha Franklin and Annie Lennox)

Vacation *(The Go-Go's)*

Our Lips Are Sealed *(The Go-Go's)*

Car Song *(Elastica)*

Little Red Corvette *(Prince)*

Supa-Dupa Fly *(Missy Elliott)*

Holiday *(Madonna)*

Express Yourself *(Madonna)*

Ray of Light *(Madonna)*

Down That Road *(Sharon Nelson)*

Driving (dance remix) *(Everything but The Girl)*

Free (remix) *(Denice Williams)*

Dreams (remix) *(Gabrielle)*

Ladies' Night *(Lil Kim, Missy Elliott, et al.)*

Don't Fence Me In *(David Byrne)*

Don't Leave Me This Way *(Thelma Houston)*

Genius of Love *(Tom Tom Club)*

I Get Around *(Beach Boys)*

Bad Girls *(Donna Summer)*

The Wanderer *(Donna Summer)*

She Works Hard for the Money *(Donna Summer)*

Green Light *(Bonnie Raitt)*

Road Tunes

Me & the Boys *(Bonnie Raitt)*

The Road's My Middle Name *(Bonnie Raitt)*

Pink Cadillac *(Natalie Cole)*

Girls Just Wanna Have Fun *(Cyndi Lauper)*

Ease on Down the Road *(from* The Wiz*)*

On the Road Again *(Willie Nelson)*

I Will Survive *(Gloria Gaynor)*

You Can Exit *(Gloria Gaynor)*

Anybody Wanna Party? *(Gloria Gaynor)*

I'm So Excited *(Pointer Sisters)*

Takin' It to the Streets *(The Doobie Brothers)*

Break Away *(Alicia Bridges)*

Celebration *(Kool & the Gang)*

Built for Speed *(Stray Cats)*

Rev It Up & Go *(Stray Cats)*

Rock This Town *(Stray Cats)*

Losing My Religion *(R.E.M.)*

Trip on Love *(Des'ree)*

I Ain't Movin' *(Des'ree)*

Living in the City *(Des'ree)*

Where Have All the Cowboys Gone? *(Paula Cole)*

Shake Your Groove Thing *(Peaches & Herb)*

Finally *(CeCe Peniston)*

Girls *(Tina Turner)*

Two People *(Tina Turner)*

Break Every Rule *(Tina Turner)*

Born to Run *(Bruce Springsteen)*

Thunder Road *(Bruce Springsteen)*

Glory Days *(Bruce Springsteen)*

Born in the U.S.A. *(Bruce Springsteen)*

Your Good Girl's Gonna Go Bad *(Tammy Wynette)*

Anything by the *Crash Test Dummies*

The Don't-Leave-Home-Without-It List:

Even if you're a hard-core road sister, you don't want to get busted without the right paperwork or stranded without a spare tire and a jack. Don't leave home without checking off everything on this list.

* driver's license
* vehicle registration
* cash card
* credit card that's not maxed out
* phone number of a friend or relative with deep pockets and fast access to Western Union
* Swiss Army knife (with bottle opener and corkscrew)
* spare tire
* lug wrench and jack
* AAA membership card
* sunglasses
* sunblock (for left arm)
* chap stick
* bandanna
* baseball cap
* bottled water (for you or your car)

 If you're a AAA member, you can get discounts at motels across the country, free towing service if your car breaks down, *and* AAA will pay up to $200 of your bail for certain out-of-state moving violations.

 In New Mexico, women are forbidden to appear unshaven in public.

just diagnosed with a stress-related skin disease.   It's time to hit the road when

The Don't-Leave-Home-With-It List:

Okay, you've got the bare essentials together. But if you haven't unloaded your inhibitions, prejudices, and emotional baggage, you're not ready to go. You may get hundreds of miles from home, but you'll still feel trapped. As you check each one off the list, say good-bye.

* photo of boyfriend
* employee ID
* calorie-counting booklet
* pager
* laptop
* makeup
* datebook/organizer
* watch
* hair dryer
* anything that needs to be ironed

 If you have children, don't ever bring them with you. It's so easy to lose small things on the road.

you feel too fat to go to your gym. It's time to hit the road when you begin to look

There's nothing worse than being whipped senseless by high-speed hair. If you have long hair, you can handle the problem by making a ponytail holder out of a condom or a pantyliner (just peel off the backing and wrap the sticky side around your ponytail). If you have short hair, you can hold your flapping bangs in place with two pantyliners (sticky side against your hair) or just don a pair of clean undies like a shower cap and you're set.

For the Totally Neurotic Road Worrier:

If your idea of living on the edge is steering with one hand, then you may want to pack a few extras.

* jumper cables
* flashlight
* blanket
* flares
* cell phone
* sponge in a Ziploc bag
* road atlas
* empty gas can

BIG TIP If you're paranoid about running out of gas or your gas gauge is unreliable, then carry a gas can with you—but be sure it's *empty*. You'll be tempted to keep it full, which makes sense until you stop and realize that a tank of gas is a firebomb waiting to happen. It really isn't safe anywhere, even tied to the luggage rack where a flicked cigarette butt or impact friction from a high-altitude bird dropping could set it off and set your car on fire.

The Bad Girl's Tool Kit:

To take your badness to the bone, you'll need a few special tools. Pack these items in a small duffel bag with a waterproof lining (it doubles as an ice chest). Because space is tight, anything you take with you should have at least five different functions. So use it or lose it. Throughout this book, you'll find lots of wacky ways to use each of the items in your tool kit.

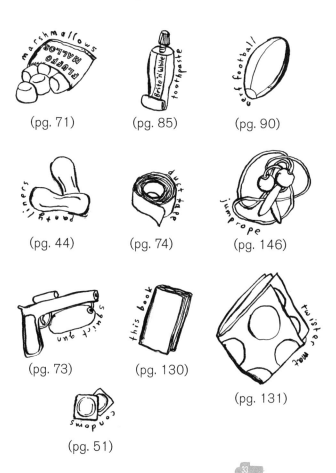

marshmallows FLUFFO MALLOS
(pg. 71)

Brite'n'White toothpaste
(pg. 85)

Nerf football
(pg. 90)

pantyliners
(pg. 44)

duct tape
(pg. 74)

jump rope
(pg. 146)

squirt gun
(pg. 73)

this book
(pg. 130)

twister mat
(pg. 131)

makeup
(pg. 51)

Tales from the Road

Incredible find at a secondhand store this afternoon. My disposable clothes smelled so bad I needed a new outfit, and pronto. I found this sweet royal-blue sequined twirler's uniform in the five-dollar bin, including blue gloves and white tasseled boots. It fit like a glove. The lady at the store asked if I was twirling at the football game tonight. Without skipping a beat, I said yes. In town I bought a baton and a pair of suntan-colored pantyhose and then scouted out the high school. When I got there, the stands were already packed. It was a big game between the Devils (my team) and the Matadors. Near the end of the first half, I slipped out of the stands and headed over to the end of the track where the other twirlers were warming up. When the band started marching onto the field for the half-time extravaganza, I marched right out there with them and improvised my own spectacularly lousy routine. When we marched off the field, I was promptly cut from the squad by the twirling captain, who was not the least bit amused. But I was invited to the post-game dance by a nice boy carrying a trombone.

what to wear

Never pack a lot of clothes—it's just not worth the trouble. Trying to decide on a new outfit every morning is way too stressful on the road. Choose a look before you leave and go with it for the duration. What you wear should depend on your desired mood (good) and attitude (bad).

You can go as you are, but it's much more fun to go as you're not. When you wear the kinds of clothes you don't normally wear at home, you'll feel liberated and free to be bad—whatever that means to you. If you always wear jeans, try pumps and a little black dress. If you're normally a prep, go punk. If you're always perfectly put together, dress like a slob. If you're a slave to fashion, set yourself free and wear the oldest rags in your giveaway bag. On the road, comfort is king, but style is queen.

BIG TIP Don't pack anything when you road trip—just shop sale racks or thrift stores and drop your disposable clothes along the way. Be creative and leave your underwear someplace outrageous—under a bar stool, in a mailbox, in the microwave at a convenience store. It's the ultimate leave-behind. You may not be in anyone's sexual fantasies, but at least your panties will be.

Road-Trip Personas

If you're not sure who you want to be or what to wear, try on these inspiring personas. Maybe one will fit just right.

The Garbo:

The look: Glamorous and aloof.

The outfit: A trench coat, dark glasses, and a scarf over your head.

The attitude: I *vant* to be alone.

The destination: Dollywood, to reflect on fame and ride the spinning E cups.

Thelma & Louise:

The look: Rugged yet feminine.

The outfit: Jeans, cowboy boots, and a sleeveless shirt.

The attitude: Treat me nice or I'll blow you away.

The destination: FBI headquarters for the tour and a little target practice.

The Just Bobbit:

The look: Angry and crazed.

The outfit: Flannel pajamas and an overcoat with a big kitchen knife in the pocket

The attitude: Cut it out or I'll cut it off.

The destination: The Sausage Capital (Frankfort, Kentucky) to job hunt.

Bonnie without Clyde:

The look: Armed and dangerous.

The outfit: A black beret, a belted leather coat and a violin case.

The attitude: Live free or cry.

The destination: Any small town in the Midwest to open a bank account.

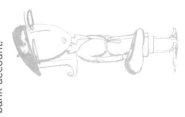

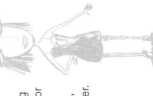

Take This Job and Shove It:

The look: Burned out and beady-eyed.
The outfit: Sweats and sneakers.
The attitude: I'm outa here.
The destination: Austin, Texas, to drink coffee and smoke filterless cigarettes.

The Fugitive:

The look: Hunted and haggard.
The outfit: Anything dirty, sweaty, and torn.
The attitude: Suspicious of everything and everyone.
The destination: Alcatraz Island for a quick tour of prison accommodations.

I'm Driving As Fast As I Can:

The look: Defeated and depressed.
The outfit: Pajamas, a bathrobe, and fuzzy slippers.
The attitude: Could it get any worse?
The destination: The Mall of America for some serious retail therapy.

Mad Maxine:

The look: Menacing and fast.
The outfit: Motorcycle boots and lots of skintight black leather.
The attitude: Take no prisoners.
The destination: Washington, D.C., to run down Jesse Helms.

Sleazy Rider:

The look: Sexy and spent.
The outfit: A little black dress, ripped stockings, and stiletto heels.
The attitude: I'm not looking for Mr. Right—I'm looking for Mr. Right Now.
The destination: Las Vegas, to do whatever and whoever.

where to go

Go anywhere that sounds like fun. Set out to visit a "Legendary Landmark" that you've never seen before—the Grand Canyon, the Statue of Liberty, Niagara Falls, or the Golden Gate Bridge. Head in the general direction of a "Divine Destination"—Graceland, the Liberace Museum, or Lizzie Borden's House. Aim for a "Funky Festival" that sounds therapeutic—the Mermaid Parade on Coney Island in New York; the Testicle Festival in Clinton, Montana; or the Ostrich Races in Chandler, Arizona. But you don't have to have a destination or even a plan in mind. You can just hit the open road, put the pedal to the metal, and see where you end up.

BIG TIP Check out the directory of Legendary Landmarks, Divine Destinations, Excellent Events, and Funky Festivals at the back of this book.

When your need for escape can be summarized in a word and you're not sure where to go, just take the **Instant Destination Diagnostic Test.**

add things you've already done to your "to do" list just to cross them off. It's time

Instant Destination Diagnostic Test

If You're Feeling	Head For
trapped	Freedom, California
old	Dinosaur, Colorado
despondent	Hope, Arkansas
sick	Doctor Phillips, Florida
pimply	Rocky Face, Georgia
sinful	Eden, Idaho
defeated	Triumph, Louisiana
short	Dwarf, Kentucky
dirty	Bath, Maine
lonely	Friendsville, Maryland
dumb	Braintree, Massachusetts
tired	Coffee, Tennessee
ugly	Beauty, Kentucky
needy	Needmore, Tennessee
empty	Nothing, Arizona
fat	Butts, Georgia
unloved	Loves Park, Illinois
bored	Challenge, California
dependent	Independence, Kansas

to hit the road when your therapist down-sizes and lets you go. It's time to hit the

are you my motor?
(Basic Auto Maintenance)

One of the thrills of road tripping is knowing that anything could go wrong at any given moment: a blowout, a burnout, loss of wiper fluid, loss of cabin pressure . . . the possibilities are endless. But if you poke around under the hood and kick a few tires every now and then, you can often prevent impending disaster. And you'll score points with the local gas station guy, who will think you know what you're doing.

Preventive Medicine

Here are a few things to look for (if you haven't a clue, see diagram):

Radiator:

Function: The radiator is that thing with a cap right behind the grille. It keeps your car from overheating by circulating the liquid in the cooling system through a series of water channels.

Check the fluid level in the plastic holding tank connected to the radiator (look for the fill line). See if the tank is full enough and the liquid is pretty clear. If it's rusty or has crap floating around in it, change it. Older cars don't have the plastic bottle, so you'll have to wait until the engine cools down, then carefully unscrew the

road when you've been researching cryogenics on the Internet.   It's time to hit the

cap. The fluid level should be a couple of inches below the opening. If it's lower than that, add some water.

While you're at it, cop a feel along the hoses coming in and out of the radiator. If they're leaking, cracked, squishy, or otherwise grossing you out, they probably need to be replaced.

Fan Belt:

Function: The fan belt connects the *fan* and the *alternator*. When you turn on the engine, the engine turns the fan. The fan turns the belt, which drives the alternator, which generates electricity to run the electrical system.

About every 2,500 miles, check to see if the fan belt is cracked, frayed, or gives more than half an inch. If you see a problem, have the belt replaced or tightened—or you may not be able to start your car.

> **BIG TIP** If your fan belt breaks while you're driving through the middle of nowhere, you can replace it temporarily with the waistband cut off of a pair of tights or panty hose (as you'd expect, Lycra works best). The elastic ribbing provides just enough bite to hold it in place.

road when you have an overpowering need to sleep in a tepee. It's time to hit the

Q: What 1960s car did Ralph Nader describe as "unsafe at any speed" and why?
A: GM's Corvair, because the engine was in the rear

Battery:

Function: The battery is that big black box on the side that's filled with a water-and-acid solution and probably has crusty stuff on top. It stores electricity, which is generated by the alternator and sent to all the parts of the car that run electrically.

Open the battery caps or bars on the top of the battery. If you can see the tops of the plates inside the battery, add distilled water. If you see a lot of crusty, cruddy acid deposits on top of the battery, brush them off or pour a little Coke or Pepsi over it. (That eats away the deposits in minutes and may kill your cola cravings.) Look for other warning signs, like frayed or broken cables, dirt, water, loose bolts, cracked case, corrosion, and other sickly symptoms.

Hoses:

Function: If you don't know what a hose is, you probably shouldn't be driving. Squeeze all the hoses under the hood and check for loose connections, leaks, cracks, bulges, and squishes. If something hisses at you or squirts in your face, replace it.

BIG TIP In a pinch, leaky hoses can be repaired using a variety of spare items you might have in the car. Try using some chewing gum or tinfoil as a patch and wrap it around the hose and secure it with duct tape, dental floss, a rubber band, or a condom. Let your imagination run wild.

road when you buy your first set of wheels.   It's time to hit the road when another

Oil:

Function: Oil to a car is like a road trip to the human brain. One prevents the other from drying up, overheating, rusting, catching fire, and exploding. Motor oil lubricates and cools the moving parts of the engine and reduces a buildup of rust and corrosion. To check the oil, first find the dipstick. It's that little thing with the ring on the end of it down at the side of your engine (see diagram on page 41). Wait until your engine has been shut off for a few minutes, then pull out the dipstick and wipe it clean with whatever you have handy (a fast-food wrapper or pantyliner works if you can't find a rag). Shove the dipstick back into the little hole, then pull it out again. Look for the "add" and "full" indicators on the end of the dipstick and see how much of it is covered with the film of oil. If it's only at the "add," then unscrew the cap on the top of the engine—*not* the radiator cap—then pour a quart of oil in the hole with the aid of a funnel, and thank God that you had this book along to tell you to add oil when the dipstick reads "add." Note: The oil should be the color of molasses. If it looks black and gooky, it needs to be changed.

 Motor oil is kind of like sunscreen—it comes in different weights and grades for different climates: 20/50 oil is thicker and better in cold climates, 10/30 oil is thinner and better in hot climates, 10/40 oil is the standard and always a safe bet. (Warning: Do not use motor oil as a sunscreen.)

 For best engine performance, change your fluids and filters more often than you change your hair color.

Things to do with . . . Pantyliners

* keep that one pair of underwear smelling fresh for days
* stick to a hot coffee cup for insulation
* stick to a cold cup to keep your inner thighs from freezing

* absorb excess moisture when you're forced to drip dry or there's a long line for the bathroom
* wet it, stick it to your hand, and clean the inside of the windshield
* use as Post-it notes: write a message and stick to windshield
* wipe off the dipstick when checking the oil
* use with duct tape as a bandage on an open wound
* wet with ice-cold water and stick to the inside of a baseball cap to stay cool
* stick over your eyes and use as a "beauty sleep" mask
* use as a ponytail holder (works great until it's time to let your hair down)

bridesmaid dress and matching pumps. It's time to hit the road when your date

before you hit the road

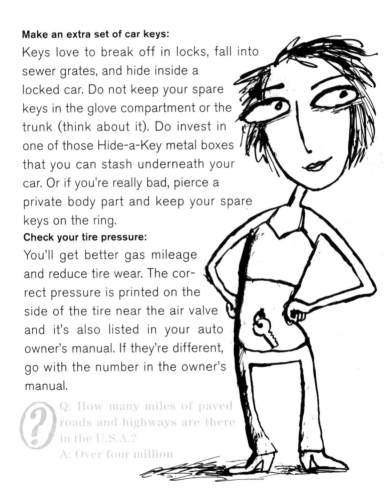

Make an extra set of car keys:

Keys love to break off in locks, fall into sewer grates, and hide inside a locked car. Do not keep your spare keys in the glove compartment or the trunk (think about it). Do invest in one of those Hide-a-Key metal boxes that you can stash underneath your car. Or if you're really bad, pierce a private body part and keep your spare keys on the ring.

Check your tire pressure:

You'll get better gas mileage and reduce tire wear. The correct pressure is printed on the side of the tire near the air valve and it's also listed in your auto owner's manual. If they're different, go with the number in the owner's manual.

Q: How many miles of paved roads and highways are there in the U.S.A.?
A: Over four million

makes a call from his cellular phone in the middle of dinner. It's time to hit the

Dry, chapped skin can be a problem on the road, especially when you're traveling with the top down. Fortunately, you can load up on an excellent moisturizer for free at any fast-food joint or convenience store—mayonnaise. Don't knock it till you've tried it! A dime-size dollop is all you need for smooth, soft hands. Just rub it in like any hand lotion and rinse with a little water afterward. Mayo moisturizes dry arms and legs too. You may smell a bit tangy and attract a few flies, but that's a small price to pay for beauty.

Check the key fluids in your car:

★ Fill the tank with gas. (If you have to stop for gas before crossing your county line, you may get sucked back into the responsibility vortex and turn back.)

★ Check the oil. (An engine fire is a not a good way to end your trip.)

★ Fill up on windshield-wiper fluid. (Staring at a live, flapping bug splat can lead to years of trauma therapy.)

★ Check the coolant level. (It's the stuff that circulates through the radiator and keeps your engine from overheating.)

Remove your wedding ring:

Why risk losing it—or all those free-drink opportunities—along the way?

On the Road

2

*A*t last, you're in the car, roaring down the road. Maybe you have a destination in mind, maybe not. The engine's purring, the stereo's blasting your favorite tunes, you feel the wind on your face and it smells like freedom. You forget about finding the perfect job, the perfect diet, the perfect wardrobe, the perfect relationship. The world you see through the windshield comes at you like an action movie. You get a rush of adrenaline—you're the heroine.

Now is the time to unleash your inner wild and explore your secret desires to be bad. Go ahead, break your own rules, be raunchy, racy, fast, and free. No matter who you are or how you live at home, the badder you are on the road, the better you'll feel.

The first step to badness is understanding the relationship between you and your car. If you're like most women, you've been conditioned to think of a car as a mobile chatroom, or a big purse on wheels, or even a high-speed motorized shopping cart. There's a hole for gas, a hole for the key, a steering wheel, and a stereo. That's all you need to know. But a car is much more than that—it's your freedom fighter, your power booster, your ticket to ride. It's a stimulant, an antidepressant, and a *vroom* with a view.

No matter what you drive, your car is a powerful performance machine built to fulfill your need for speed. Under the hood is a perfectly engineered system that will respond to your slightest movement and desire. Floor it and feel the thrust of acceleration and the surge of exhilaration. Don't be afraid to admit you've got a taste for torque or piston envy. When you're in the driver's seat, all the horsepower under the hood is yours.

To really tap into that power, practice aggressive driving—gun the engine, make a few erratic lane changes, tailgate, and speed. Better yet, try **passive-aggressive driving**. Once you feel the power surge through you, there's no turning back.

passive-aggressive driving v *maneuvering with deliberate yet subtle hostility (i.e., floor it and pass a car on the right, then pull back into the lane, slow down, and wave at the driver behind you)*

surrounding your house. It's time to hit the road when your boyfriend has just run

finding your badness

You don't have to break the law to be bad. There are degrees of badness and endless ways of being bad. It all depends on you and your idea of good behavior. If you're not sure how to begin, ask yourself what you'd love to do but don't ever allow yourself to do at home. Start gradually and ease into it. Show a little road rage. Drink regular instead of decaf. Eat a double cheeseburger and large fries—and enjoy them without any guilt. At the next stop, pick up some blue eye shadow and a frosted coral lipstick, then use a restaurant bathroom without ordering anything, and help yourself to a fistful of mints on your way out the door. Just open yourself up to the possibilities and let your badness grow.

If you're suffering a badness block, **do the dog** or put on some empowering headwear. Anything goofy will loosen you up. Wear a Burger King bag, a clean pair of underwear, or a red inflated condom on your head.

do the dog v *1: to stick your head far out of a car window, facing forward with your nose high in the air 2: to show great joy*

Things to do with . . . Condoms

(Non-lubricated condoms offer greater versatility, but lubricated give you a spa-quality moisturizing hand treatment.)

* have safe sex
* blow up, knot, and use as a pillow, headrest, or lumbar back support
* snakebite tourniquet
* tampon disposal bag
* ponytail holder or headband
* change purse when you're wearing a bikini
* grifter's tool ("I found this used condom in my sheets and I refuse to pay for this room." Add a little mayo to close the deal.)
* fill with crushed ice and use as a cold pack
* refill container for liquid soap, ketchup, and other roadside freebies
* inflate a bunch, twist into balloon animals to sell to small children
* high-speed water balloon fights

off with your brother. It's time to hit the road when your parents are getting a

Bitchin' Bad Habits

Developing a few new bad habits is an excellent way to get in touch with your badness. Here are three proven winners that will get you in the mood for a bad attitude.

Burning Rubber:

Despite what you may have heard, burning rubber is *not* really hot sex. It's better. It's that ear-piercing screech that happens when some obnoxious jerk peels out, leaving behind a cloud of stinky smoke and a bunch of people shaking their heads. It's bad for your car, and bad for the environment, but it feels so good!

Burning rubber is right up there with road tripping as a classic American tradition. Ever since the beginning of "car time," **doin' a burnie** has been the fastest, fiercest way of announcing to everyone within earshot, "Watch out! I'm bad!" Typically this has been guy territory. But those days are over. If you're feeling bad, now's the time to let the world know. Some will fear you, others will revere you—but no one will mess with a chick who burns rubber.

do a burnie v *1: burn rubber 2: show off 3: make an ass of yourself 4: do a guy named Bernie 5: have diarrhea*

Many genetic researchers believe there is a burning-rubber gene that is dominant in some families and nonexistent in others. Either you have it or you don't. This is right-wing propaganda. With enough practice and the

Puffy eyes from last night's bender?
Pick up a little Preparation H and apply it to
the area under your eyes. (Follow directions on
the package, well sort of.)

divorce. It's time to hit the road when your parents aren't getting a divorce but

right car, anyone can learn to burn rubber. Before you try it at a crowded intersection, practice in an empty parking lot or on a deserted street. Once you've got it down, you'll be hooked.

Automatic Burnies:

It's much easier to burn rubber driving an automatic than it is in a manual transmission. First, be sure that your seat belt is on and the emergency brake is off. Basically, all you do is keep your left foot pressed really hard on the brake pedal while you accelerate hard with your right foot. (If you had three feet, two would be on the brake and one on the gas.) When the rear wheels are rotating fast enough to achieve the desired screech and stench, quickly release the brake and keep accelerating.

Stick-shift Burnies:

You can burn rubber if you're driving a stick shift, but you have to have a really heavy clutch and a powerful engine. All you do is push in the clutch, put the car in first gear, gun the engine, then pop the clutch and hang on. If you're not getting the desired effect, you're probably not giving it enough gas. Really floor it!

Dip till You Drop:

Okay, admit it. That worn, faded circle in the back pocket of a pair of jeans looks kind of cool. The fat lip and the cup of brown spit are totally disgusting, but you've always secretly wondered, What's the deal with chewing tobacco? Here's your chance to find out. In just about any roadside store in this country, you can find a wide offering of smokeless tobacco—Skoal, Kodiac, Red Man—in flavors like wintergreen, cherry, and spearmint.

Sure lighting up a cig is fine for copping an everyday bad attitude. But chewing tobacco—or dipping as it's called in more fashionable circles—is the ultimate bad girl nic hit. You get a good rush and you look super bad doing it. It's definitely **taboo voodoo**. Like most of the finer things in life, smokeless tobacco is an acquired taste. Just take a pinch (no bigger than a raisin) and tamp it down between your cheek and gum. The first time you do it, your gum area will sting a little for about 30 seconds. But after that, you've killed off enough cells that it doesn't hurt a bit. Definitely have an empty cup or bottle handy to use as a spittoon. It's okay to swallow when dipping, but spit first so you don't swallow any saliva or tobacco juice. (The good news: your breath, hair, car, and clothes won't smell like smoke. The bad news: if you swallow tobacco juice, you'll puke.)

taboo voodoo n *that magical feeling you get when you break a social taboo*

boss. It's time to hit the road when you finally realize that the money you save by

The tobacco comes sealed in tiny gauzelike pouches that you suck on. The rush isn't as strong but you don't have to worry about overloading and having a major jit-fit or bits of tobacco floating around in your mouth and accidentally swallowing some.

Doin' Donuts:

Remember those morons in high school who squealed around and around doing donuts in the parking lot? Remember thinking, "How stupid!" Well that's the secret—doing donuts is so flat-out stupid it's a gas! Find an empty parking lot or quiet stretch of road. All you do is crank the wheel all the way to the right or the left and floor it. The driver should have her seat belt on at all times so she doesn't fly out the window. But the passengers should go without so they can appreciate the slamming fun of centrifugal force. To achieve donut nirvana, try eating donuts while doing donuts. It's a spiritual experience. But leave your hot coffee on the curb.

BIG TIP Have no idea what direction you're driving? All even-numbered U.S. interstate highways run east/west; all odd-numbered interstate highways run north/south.

 In Washington, a motorist with criminal intentions is required to stop at the city limits and telephone the police chief to inform him that he is entering the town.

bringing your lunch isn't enough to justify eating soggy sandwiches. It's time to

rules of the road trip

A road trip is the world you create where it's safe to explore your own boundaries and break all the rules you live by at home. But you want to feel safe doing that. Everyone in your car should agree to these four road-trip rules:

1. Don't hurt yourself.

2. Don't hurt anyone else.

3. What is shared on a road trip is sacred and not to be repeated back home.

4. If there are more than two road sisters, you have to call shotgun.

Calling Shotgun

Shotgun is the prized position of riding in the front seat next to the driver. Calling shotgun is an age-old practice that adds sport and skill to what is always a sensitive subject—seating arrangements.

The Rules:

1. To call shotgun, a passenger must say the word *shotgun* in a strong, clear voice. The driver must hear and acknowledge the call, verifying it for the others.

2. Shotgun can be called only when all road sisters are outside and returning to the vehicle.

3. Early calls are strictly prohibited. Specifically, calls

hit the road when you think a date is just a thing with a pit.   It's time to hit the

made inside a restaurant, bar, store, or motel will not be honored. Shotgun cannot be booked in advance under any circumstances.

4. In the case of ties and/or disputes, the driver has final say. The driver has the right to terminate shotgun privileges at any time, eject the shotgunner to the backseat, and immediately name an alternate.

Exceptions to the Rules:

1. If the owner of the vehicle is not driving, she automatically rides shotgun, unless she declines.

2. If the intended driver is drunk or otherwise impaired, then she rides shotgun or closest to the window that opens widest, whether it's in the front or back.

> **BIG TIP** When **power booting** at high speeds, always stick your head as far as possible out the window and position yourself as far back as possible. Otherwise, your sisters riding in back will never speak to you again.
>
> **power booting** v *projectile puking, hurling, barfing, blowing chunks*

road when you're afraid to get angry because someone might think you're not

Auto-erotic Secrets

A car is like a weapon:

Know how to use it safely and nobody will get hurt. Keep it locked up when you're not using it. Clean it often with a soft rag, oil it regularly, and don't ever drive it when loaded.

Mechanics wear coveralls for a reason:

Mechanics and gas station guys are not just working on cars, they're talking a secret language of love. If you don't believe it, say "Hey, baby . . ." before each of these seemingly innocent automotive phrases, and you'll see what's really going on under those coveralls.

"Hey, baby . . ."

Can you check my oil?

Smells like my engine is overheating.

It's been so long since my tires were rotated.

Fill her up?

Want to look under my hood?

I think you have the part I need.

I'm burning oil.

I really need a new hose in there.

I hope you've got chains.

Real men don't drive an automatic:
The only reason guys drive an automatic is so there is no stick shift to get in the way on a date.

Driving is like having sex:
A short, fast ride can be fun, but a long, slow ride is more memorable and far more satisfying.

A car is a huge vibrator on wheels:
All a girl really needs to get some satisfaction is a car, a tank of gas, a bumpy road, and a tight pair of jeans.

The Beauty of an Alias

At some point during your road trip, you will need an alias, so you may as well choose a good one and choose it early. There are times when a woman simply shouldn't use her real name. Trust your instincts, you'll recognize those times—singing karaoke in Nashville, trying on prom dresses in Kansas City, entering a wet T-shirt contest in Fort Lauderdale. But you don't have to be engaged in questionable or criminal activities to use an alias. It's fun anyplace, anytime. And it helps to establish your road-altered ego, which sets you apart from who you are at home.

Any name will do as long as it suits your mood and makes you feel free to misbehave. An alias can be something informative—Helen Bedd, Dora Jarr, Barb Tung, Anita Margarita—or something inspirational—Towanda Olova, Carlotta Fun, Mona Lott. Once you've got one you love, use it every chance you get. No matter what you're doing, you'll have a sense of anonymity and the comfort of knowing that you won't be tracked down easily later.

If you can't think of an alias that feels right, use the **instant alias finder** to figure out your "porn star" name, your "soap opera" name, and your "road-trip" name.

Don't let dry, rough cuticles slow you down. Just visit the dried-meat-snacks department of any roadside store and stock up on beef jerky, Slim Jims, and the like. As you eat, massage the oily residue from the jerky into your cuticles. Works better than any manicure product and tastes good too.

nice.   It's time to hit the road when your dog has more friends than you do.   It's

Instant Alias Finder

	First Name	Last Name	Examples
Your Porn Star Name	the name of your first pet	your mother's maiden name	*Muffet Moore* *Fluffy Sinclaire*
Your Soap Opera Name	your middle name	the name of the first street where you lived	*McLain Livorna* *Hall Lexington*
Your Road Trip Name	what you had for breakfast	where you last peed beside the road	*Waffles Minnesota* *Scrapple Las Vegas*

time to hit the road when you always show up at parties right on time.   It's time

On the Road, Beware of . . .

bumper thumpers n *people with a compulsive need to proclaim their convictions and "spread the word" via obnoxious bumper stickers*

countrifried adj *a delusional, temporary state in which all of your problems can be reduced to the lyrics of a country-and-western song*

Crooning Fatigue Syndrome n *vocal strain caused by hours of singing along to Top-40 songs*

driving by Braille v *excessive reliance upon the raised reflectors that mark the lines on a highway in order to stay within your lane*

Q-tips n *white-haired senior citizens driving 20 miles slower than the speed limit*

tour-ons n *the lowest and slowest form of tourist*

Tunnel-Car-Pull Syndrome n *a chronic and often debilitating syndrome that mysteriously causes your car to be pulled toward the wall when driving through a tunnel*

Q-tip :

Your Car—Fill Her Up!

Whatever you do, do not clean the inside of your car along the way. The crap that accumulates on the floor—lottery tickets, bottle caps, cigarette butts, receipts, stale onion rings, ketchup packets, tacky souvenirs, ticket stubs, matchbooks with phone numbers—will be little treasures when you get home. Just holding a winning bingo card or sniffing a fossilized French fry can give you a quick hit of freedom, enough to prevent a mental melt-down when you're back in the grind. The bigger your stash of trashy keepsakes, the better your chances of surviving road-trip withdrawal. If you're wading in crap toward the end of your journey, then throw everything into the trunk so you'll have a pile of stuff to remind you of every rude detail of your road adventure.

BIG TIP If your car heater doesn't work and you are freezing, stop at the next minimart and load up on microwavable burritos. Nuke the hell out of them and stuff them in all your pockets. When they cool down, you chow down!

to hit the road when you're about to have a birthday that will require you to lie

The Truth About Cars and Men

What the car really says about the man behind the wheel.

Acura Legend	I'm rich and too boring for German cars.
BMW	I bought my wife.
Cadillac Eldorado	I'm a pimp.
Corvette	I'm having a midlife crisis.
Dodge Dart	I'm above materialism and, by the way, I teach special ed.
El Camino	I clean pools for a living, but I've got a great bod.
Ford Crown Victoria	I love watching people slow to 55 and change lanes when I approach.

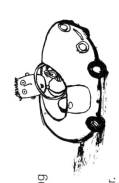

GEO Tracker	I've got a fake ID.
Honda Civic	I'm still working on my Ph.D.
Jeep Cherokee	I live in the city and love four-four-wheeling over medians.
Lincoln Town Car	I moonlight as a limo driver.
Mazda Miata	Whee! I'm Peter Pan and I'm driving Minnie Mouse's slipper!
MGB	I'm a mechanic.
Oldsmobile	I inherited this car from my mother.
Porsche	I have a two-inch penis.
Toyota Camry	I have children and no personality.
Volvo Station Wagon	I'm afraid of my wife.

Drive-by Dating

If you're afraid of intimacy, not ready for commitment, or haven't brushed your teeth in three days, drive-by dating is for you. It's best to do this on a highway or freeway, where speed keeps you at a safe distance from your "date." Just like regular dating, this game has no strict rules—which is what makes it so appealing. The object of the game is to get the guy in the other car to exit, expecting you to follow. You, of course, floor it and keep on sailing.

How you bait your hook is your business. But when you set the hook and get the guy to take the exit, be certain there isn't an on-ramp connected to the off-ramp or he'll pull right back on, and you'll have some explaining to do.

Here are a few ideas to inspire you.

Hand Signals:

Introduce yourself with a casual wave and a flirtatious smile. Then move on to more elaborate messages. Point to your eye, make a heart symbol in the air, then aim a finger at your target. Or draw in the air the letter U, and the letter R, then lick your finger, touch it to the window, and act like it's sizzling hot. You get the idea.

Car Dancing:

The fine art of car dancing is lost on most men. But with the right tunes blaring and a little help from your road sisters, you'll get him movin' and groovin' in no time. Start with a little shoulder shimmy and a head bob, then add a steady beat on the steering wheel or dashboard. When you've got your groove, throw in a few flashier moves like "The Turn Signal" (reach your left arm out and flash your fingers to the rhythm, then reach your right hand out and do the same, then alternate arms) or "The Floor It!" (throw your head and shoulders back to the beat).

Strip Driver:

Experience the thrill of strip poker without the bother of cards. A shoe for a shoe, a sock for a sock, a belt for a belt. And then some. If you show him yours, he'll show you his. So you better want to see everything you ask for—you'll get it.

It's time to hit the road when you try your first home perm. Oops.   It's time to hit

Tales from the Road

Learned an exciting new road game—strip driver—in Missouri, the "Show Me" State (it figures). I was driving west with Halle in her black Jeep Wrangler, affectionately known as the Pig. It was early in the morning. The top was off, the sun was shining down, the wind was blowing my dress up and whipping strands of hair across my face. We were feeling bad when this cowboy in a pickup pulled up next to us and started making eyes. He took off a boot and waved it provocatively. I was clueless, but Halle pulled off her cowboy boot and waved it right back. Then we saw his sock blowing in the wind. So I took off my bandanna and snapped it in his direction. Next he managed to pull off his shirt, revealing his burly chest and shoulders, which was a welcome sight but left me feeling a little overdressed. Then he took off his belt. It was time to start playing cat and mouse. I floored it, and he caught up. I hit the brakes, and he slowed down. When he finally pointed to the next exit, he looked like he wanted more than a strong cup of coffee. We just smiled and nodded enthusiastically. He took the exit, but we kept on driving and never looked back. I have to say, it was an exciting way to start the day.

Q: What year was the first coast-to-coast highway completed?
A: 1927

Other On-the-Road Activities

Actor-Movie-Actor

One person starts by saying a well-known actor's name, the next person has to respond with the name of a movie the actor was in (it doesn't have to be a leading role). In order to stay in the game, the next person has to give the name of another actor in that movie. The next player follows with a different movie that the same actor was in. And so on. The last player in the game wins.

For example:

Susan Sarandon. *Thelma & Louise.* Geena Davis. *The Accidental Tourist.* William Hurt. *Broadcast News.* Albert Brooks. *Lost in America.*

The more obscure the movies and actors, the harder it gets. If you feel really generous, you can give the nerdy, disadvantaged bookworms in your car a handicap of up to three passes per game.

> **BIG TIP** If you want to raise the stakes in any road game, try this: The winner gets to order the most disgusting thing on the menu at the next meal, and the loser has to eat it.

Mobile Marshmallow Toss

More than a fun way to pass the time on boring stretches of highway, this game is a foolproof method for making friends *or* enemies. Each player starts with a full bag of marshmallows. The winner is the first to score 100 points or the person with the highest score when all the bags are empty. (Doughnut holes can be substituted for marshmallows.)

Rules:

Marshmallows must be thrown while the car is moving in order for a hit to count. You have to call your target before and after the score. No multiple marshmallow throws allowed. No trading points for marshmallows. No joining forces with another player in the middle of a match.

Scoring:

1 point for hitting a moving car

3 points for hitting an oncoming moving car

5 points for hitting a mailbox or a road sign

10 points for hitting an open window

15 points for hitting an open sunroof

25 points for hitting a cow or a cop car

Bonus Points:

3 points for getting an angry gesture from another motorist

5 points for getting a marshmallow thrown back at you

10 points for getting someone in another vehicle to eat your marshmallow

Things to do with . . . Marshmallows

* kill an hour or two making finger taffy
    * plug a muffler hole
    * use the bag as a pillow
    * toilet paper
    * jam a parking meter
    * use dental floss and a paper clip
      to make a choker necklace
* use as press-on nipples to win a wet T-shirt
  contest
* turn your car into moving art
* juggle to make some change on a street
  corner

If you have mini-marshmallows . . .

* use them as nose plugs to
  survive unbreathable
  bathrooms
* use them as ear
  plugs when try-
  ing to nap in the
  backseat

"My First, My Worst":

Swap stories about all your titillating and humiliating first and worst experiences—first kiss, worst kiss, first sex, worst sex, first sex in a car, worst sex in a car, first road trip adventure, worst road trip adventure. It's an entertaining way to accelerate bad girl bondage or just pass the time.

Sing:

Try "99 bagels with schmear on the wall, 99 bagels with schmear" to kill even the strongest bagel cravings. (In most towns around the country you can't even find a bagel. And if you do, it's really a salty donut.)

"I Know His Secret":

Make up elaborate stories about other motorists, where they're going, and why they're driving so fast.

Or:

Write bad road haiku. Rename the glove compartment. Brainstorm new inventions. Write the sequel to *Thelma & Louise*. Share your most outrageous job resignation fantasies. Write a screenplay based on your life. Shoot squirt guns at other cars.

Things to do with . . . A Squirt Gun

* great for cooling off in a hot, sticky car
* ambush rude motorists
* fill with soda at fast-food self-serve dispensers
* use as a discreet flask
* stick under your shirt and pretend you have a gun if someone's trying to car-jack you (*Caution:* If they have a real gun, you probably don't want to try this.)
* cool off an overheating engine
* shoot down annoying bugs trapped in the car
* use as a water pick to free food from your teeth
* spot clean a stain
* loosen bug splats from the windshield and grille
* feel like a kid again
* refreshing wake-up call for sleeping passengers

 **BIG TIP** A vehicle with a gun rack always has the right of way. If both vehicles have gun racks, then the one flying the Confederate flag has the right of way.

Things to do with ... Duct Tape

* repair a cracked engine hose
* hog-tie a poorly behaved hitchhiker
* tow a car (see page 145)
* make a sun visor
* temporarily conceal license plate numbers
* pull-off bib for messy barbecue meals
* fix broken sunglasses
* use as a nose strip to remove blackheads and blocked pores
* tape up your breasts for that strapless-bra effect

your stepmother asks you to drop acid with her. It's time to hit the road when you

Old Favorite Road Games

Slug Bug (a.k.a. Punch Buggy):

The first person to spot a VW bug gets to slug another passenger in the arm.

20 Questions:

One person thinks of a famous landmark, person, thing, animal, place, or whatever. The others try to figure out what she is thinking of by asking 20 questions. Of course, the first question is always, "Animal, vegetable, or mineral?"

The License Plate Game:

Try to spot license plates from as many different states as possible. Only the first person to call out the state can add it to her collection. The player with the most license plates when everyone is dying from boredom wins.

Alphabet Game:

Starting with A, everyone tries to find all the letters of the alphabet in order. The first person to see a letter on a license plate, sign, or bumper sticker calls it, and no one else can count that same letter.

BIG TIP If you're prone to low-blood-sugar attacks, keep a box of Jell-O in the glove compartment. When you feel the shakes coming on, dip into it with a wet fingertip and suck down that sugar.

BIG TIP Discuss writing a book about road tripping for at least one minute each day, and keep all of your receipts so you can deduct the entire cost of your trip—including mileage—at tax time.

burn off your eyelashes and eyebrows while trying to light the oven pilot.   It's time

Inter-auto Communication

Whether you're driving across the state or across the country, be prepared and have at least one way to communicate with other drivers. (Giving the **one-finger salute** is effective but rather limiting.) You never know when you'll need a quick way to vent your road rage, talk safety, or just say no.

one-finger salute v 1: to show anger, disapproval or disrespect 2: to flip the bird 3: to give the finger

Sign Language:

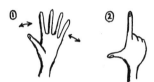

Wave bye-bye, then make a letter L with your thumb and index finger.

[Get Lost, Loser]

Point to the other driver, mimic holding a steering wheel, then pinch your nose.

[You Drive Stinky]

 In Tennessee, it is against the law to shoot any game other than whales from a moving automobile.

to hit the road when you're still hosting *Melrose* parties. It's time to hit the road

Flash Cards:

Spiral-bound index cards or a notebook work quite well. If you want to be able to wave your cards, duct tape the cover to a hairbrush or flare.

[I'm Brain-Douching Now. Ask Me How.]
[Your Car Is On Fire]

Magnetic Letters:

Unless your car has a fiberglass body, magnetic letters will stick on a car door as well as they do on a fridge. You can pick up a set at a toy store, variety store, or even a supermarket.

[U IDIOT RU BLIND]
[LETS DV8]

Dry Board Markers:

Dry markers work great on the windshield or windows, and your message easily wipes clean with a dry panty-liner (peel off the backing and stick it to your hand). Practice writing in reverse on the windshield so drivers can read your words in their rearview mirror as you gain on them.

[Danger: Women On The Verge]
[Out Of My Way I'm A Bad Girl]

Note in a Marshmallow:

Need to send a love letter, hate mail, or give complicated directions to someone in another car? No problem. Just scribble your note on a gum wrapper or scrap of paper, then jam it through the middle of a marshmallow and throw it into their car. No matter what you've written, they'll be impressed.

Great Ideas Just

Roadside services I'd like to see:

drive-thru sushi

drive-thru superstores

drive-thru therapy

drive-thru petting zoo

drive-thru orgasm and pedicure

Waiting to Happen

Things I'd like to see:

airbag piñatas

Road-trippin' Barbie

vibrator key chains

margarita Slurpees

microwave glove compartments

dashboard coffeemaker

Books I'd like to write:

Women Who Run Over Wolves

The Road More or Less Traveled

Zen and the Art of Menstrual Cycle
    Maintenance

Car of the Soul

I'm Away, You're Away

Wherever You Go, There You Are with Bad Hair

common breakdowns
and how to deal

Flat Tire:

There are two types of flat tires: the slow leak and the blowout. The blowout is a thrill. You'll hear a loud explosion accompanied by a swerving of the car toward the blown tire, and a loud thumping as your tire rotates on the rim. If your powers of perception haven't been weakened by too many hours on the road, you can identify a slow leak by a steady pulling of the car to one side. Both scenarios suck and both require immediate attention: change the tire.

What you'll need:

jack, either a tripod or scissors type
a lug wrench

What to do:

1. Try to park the car on level ground, a safe distance from speeding traffic. If you're on a hill, coast to the bottom before attempting to change the tire. If you're on a city street, turn the wheels toward the curb to prevent it from rolling away. At the very least, make sure that no one is in the car and there are no innocent passengers, bystanders, or animals near the car (unless it's someone you've been dying to flatten).

2. Block the wheels. Even if you're on level ground, grab a few rocks, a platform shoe, or any other heavy

objects you can find to wedge against the wheels at the opposite end of the car.

3. Make sure the car's in park or neutral and that the emergency brake is on before you jack it up.

4. Place the jack under the car near the flat tire so it will touch either the car frame or that big bar that supports the front- or rear-wheel suspension.

5. Remove the hubcap by prying it off with the flat end of the lug wrench or any other flat instrument. Please note: A hubcap's primary function is cosmetic, so it can come in handy in a variety of situations—use it to block the wheels or as a chip-and-dip tray for that unplanned roadside cocktail party.

6. Loosen the lug nuts (those big honkers that look like nipples and hold the wheel in place). But do not remove them until you've finished jacking up the car. This can take a little muscle, especially if they've been tightened with a power tool. If you're on the right side of the car, turn the nuts counterclockwise to loosen them. If you're on the left side of the car, look at the center of the lug to see if it has an "R" (turn clockwise) or an "L" (turn counterclockwise). If it has no letter, turn it counterclockwise. If the lugs are on so tight they won't budge, don't be afraid to stand on the lug wrench and use your full weight to loosen them.

Lost your eye shadow in a poker game three states back? Not to worry. Just rub the end of your finger against the side of a tire and then dab a little over each eye. Blend thoroughly. It comes right off with soap and water, most of the time.

7. Jack it up. Relax, breathe deeply, and apply nice even strokes. (A good workout for the biceps, triceps, and lats.) Once the car's up, give it a wiggle to make sure it's not going to come crashing down on your head.

8. *Now* remove the lug nuts. (Put them in a hubcap or a pocket so you don't accidentally kick them into a sewer grate.) Grab the flat tire and pull it toward you until it slides off the bolts. (Caution: it's heavier than it looks.) Then replace it with the spare. (If you can't find it, check the trunk, underneath the car, or the owner's manual.)

9. Tighten the lugs, put the hubcap back on with a good whack, and you're ready to rock and roll.

10. Remember: Spares are spares and usually aren't worth squat. You'll probably want to replace it with a new tire or get the flat tire fixed as soon as possible. If your spare looks like a mini bike wheel, don't cry. It will work, but it's designed to be used for short distances at a limited speed. If you have one of these cheapo numbers, check your car manual for details.

Overheating:

This is a roadside classic. You're in the middle of nowhere, the mercury's pushin' 110, and the sun's blazing down on the hood of your car. Is that a **mental mirage** or steam seeping up from the hood? Probably steam.

mental mirage n *a personal fantasy, often sexual in nature, induced by high-speed motion*

recycling your old boyfriends.   It's time to hit the road when you're saving up for

What you'll need:

water

What to do:

1. Shut off the AC and open your windows to decrease the load on the engine.

2. Check the temperature gauge on the dash, which is usually useless. If the car continues to overheat, turn on the heater full blast. This draws heat away from the engine and, unfortunately, blows it into your face.

3. If you're in stop-and-go traffic and the temperature gauge is still rising, shift into neutral and rev the engine a little bit to cool things off. And don't ride the brakes; keep some distance between you and the car ahead.

4. If the car's turning into a pressure cooker, pull off the road, open the hood, and let it cool off. Whatever you do, *don't open the radiator cap* unless you want an instant chemical face peel from a boiling geyser of radiator fluid. *Don't add water* until the car has cooled down. This should take about as long as a good pee and pie.

If you're driving in extreme heat and the car simply stops without steaming, you may be experiencing vapor lock. This happens when the gas begins boiling in the fuel line. Simply pull over and drape a wet rag (a T-shirt or a pair of undies will work nicely) on the fuel line or just wait until it cools off itself. If you've got any leftover tinfoil in the car, wrap it around the fuel line once it cools off to keep it from locking again. If not, wrap the wet rag around the line and hold in place with duct tape.

Q: What was used to steer cars before 1904, when steering wheels were added?

A: A tiller rod

a liposuction and a boob job. It's time to hit the road when you buy a puppy just

Wiper Blade Wimp Out:

A wimpy wiper blade can ruin your view and be a safety hazard. If you've got visibility problems, jump out into the rain or snow armed with a Swiss Army knife, detach the blade from the arm of the wiper, and sharpen both edges of the rubber blade with quick strokes as if you were sharpening a kitchen knife in a late-night infomercial.

Muffler Malaise:

The sole function of the muffler is to control the noise of the exhaust gases before they are released into the air through the exhaust pipe. So don't sweat it if your muffler has a hole or you scrape the whole thing off flying over a speed bump. You'll just have to put up with the embarrassing noise and possibly suffer through getting a ticket from a small-town cop with nothing better to do. If the muffler is dragging, you can easily crawl under the car and reattach it using a wire hanger, duct tape, or whatever you happen to have around. Holes can be temporarily fixed with a large wad of gum, a decal from a souvenir shop or trading post, or a Chicken McNugget. (The latter is probably the most durable. It won't melt or break apart.) Use your imagination here, there's not much that can go wrong.

Things to do with . . . Toothpaste

(use paste, not gel)

* spread on nose as substitute
  for zinc oxide to prevent
  sunburn
* make fierce war paint
* dab on tongue to freshen breath
* rub on cuts, sores, or bites instead of
  calamine lotion
* use as a deep-cleaning face mask after a
  sweaty day on the road
* brush teeth before a kissing contest
* dab above upper lip to survive a particularly
  nasty bathroom
* artfully dot the sides of the car with your
  favorite constellations or trim your windshield
  with scallops (This is fun to do to someone
  else's car too.)
* glue your favorite souvenirs to the dashboard

your parents. It's time to hit the road when you vacuum the house for exercise.

Art Cars

While the contemporary art world has been slow to recognize this emerging form of art, art cars rule the road. An art car is any vehicle that has been transformed into a moving work of art. If you're lucky enough to see one on the road, you too will be moved.

Art cars run the gamut from monothematic works, such as the *Mondrian Mobile,* to far more complex concepts involving intricate bumper-to-bumper installations—cars completely covered with living sod, old buttons, corks, cast-off golf shoes, or astro turf. As with other forms of art, certain art cars can put the viewer in peril. If you're driving at night, beware of the mobile mirrored ball, a vehicle covered with tiny reflective squares. This type of art car is mesmerizing, but it can be a disco-disaster waiting to happen, the meaning of which you'll be able to ponder for weeks while in traction. Wherever you go, keep your eyes open for art cars. They exist only for those who see them.

Transform Your Car Into an Art Car

If the muse finds you on the road, it's easy to turn your vehicle into an art car for the duration of your trip. The possibilities are endless. Here are a few suggestions to get your creative juices flowing.

Water-Based Paints:
Remember the stuff you used in grade school? It still exists. You can get it in all sorts of bright colors,

and it washes off with soap and water. Paint a mural of all your road adventures as you go or just express yourself.

Glue Gun:

For about 12 dollars, you can pick up a battery-operated glue gun in any hardware store or large drugstore. With a hot glue gun you can cover your car with Kleenex flowers and pretend you're the homecoming queen. Or use it to stick on marshmallows, French fries, chicken nuggets, tampons, or anything else that will hold at high speeds. When you get home (or get sick of what you've created), just peel the glue beads right off.

Ketchup Graffiti:

A squirt bottle borrowed from a café or diner does the trick. Be sure to give the ketchup some time to dry or the message will smear and your car will look like a menstruation mobile. (Don't try this with mustard, it could leave a mark.)

Make a Political Statement:

Burn all your bras and tie the melted mess that's left to the car antenna, luggage rack, and bumper. Then burn rubber everywhere you go.

emergency body work

A life-affirming road trip can be thigh-affirming too. A little impromptu exercise while you drive fights On-the-road Lard-ass Syndrome, relieves stiff and achy muscles from sitting in a car all day, and helps you bust a move if you're backed up after **eating down the food chain**. These road-tested exercises are about feeling better—not looking better. And they're fun. Whether you're in excellent shape or pear shape, you'll notice the difference.

eating down the food chain v *eating at less and less expensive places along the road*

Nerf Football Squeezes:

Can be performed by a driver or passenger at any speed. (Not a smart idea in traffic.) Place the Nerf football between your thighs. Slowly squeeze inward as far as possible and then release gradually. For optimum results, resist in both directions. Passing motorists may wonder what you're up to, so be sure to smile seductively and wave.

Recommended workout: Three sets of 20 or hold the squeeze until you've passed three billboards, then release for two.

Muscle group worked: Groin and glutes.

Benefit: Firms inner thighs and ass.

Nerf Football Presses:

Can be performed by a driver or passenger at any speed. Hold the Nerf football between your hands so the ends touch your palms. Slowly press inward as far as possible and then release gradually. Can be performed in three positions: in front of your chest, in front of your head (very exciting if you're driving), or behind your head.

Recommended workout: Three sets of 20 or hold the squeeze for one song on the radio, then release.

Muscle group worked: (Front presses) pectorals and deltoids; (back presses) biceps and deltoids.

Benefit: Develops chest and upper arms; increases your chances of scoring in drive-by dating.

Jog the Dog:

This passenger workout requires a cooperative if not sadistic driver. (Best on deserted back roads.) One person gets out of the car—willingly or unwillingly—and the driver takes off like a bat out of hell. The person left behind is the "yo-yo." The driver's objective is to accelerate for 25 to 50 yards, then stop and wait patiently as the yo-yo approaches, then accelerate again—always

Toothpaste not only keeps teeth clean and breath fresh, it also dries up **intranzits** overnight (just dab where you need it) and works like zinc oxide to protect your nose from the sun. **intranzit** n *a pimple caused by too many roadside burgers and fries*

hit the road when you start ironing your jeans. It's time to hit the road when you

Things to do with . . . A Nerf Football

* use as a pillow or headrest when you need to catch some z's
* bite, squeeze, pound against the dashboard when other drivers or fellow passengers are bugging the shit out of you
* cut in half and stuff each half in your bra if you get the urge for an instant boob job
* roll it under your bare feet to relieve gas pedal cramps or roll it along your spine to ease back pain
* a guy-catching antenna ornament
* put it under your shirt and pretend you're pregnant so you can cut to the front of lines or get faster service
* when you're craving physical contact, play roadside touch football with a bunch of guys
* use it as a huge curler to achieve big hair

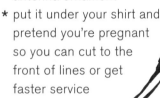

staying just out of the yo-yo's reach. The yo-yo's objective is to get back into the car. Whether the yo-yo walks, jogs, or sprints, this is an effective aerobic workout—and particularly thrilling when it comes as a surprise to the yo-yo. Taunts from other passengers or the driver increase the calorie burn.

Recommended workout: About a mile, or until the yo-yo bursts into tears or heads off the road and into a bar.

Muscle group worked: All leg muscles.

Benefit: The cardiovascular effect of a series of wind sprints; revenge.

Biteable-Butt Clenches:

Best for passengers, this can cause erratic changes in speed if performed by the driver. Squeeze your butt tight, tight, tight, like nothing's ever going in or out again, then release. Clenches can be done in rapid fire or held for a predetermined duration. In either case, go for the burn.

Recommended workout: Rapid-fire sets—squeeze and relax your butt as quickly as you can until you see a dead animal on or beside the road. Rest for 60 seconds, then repeat. Duration sets—hold a tight squeeze until you've passed either a burger joint, a cow, or a sign containing the letter P (for pucker).

Muscle group worked: Glutes and hamstrings.

Benefit: Tones backs of thighs and ass; allows for a little air between you and the hot vinyl seat.

 THE LAW In Kansas, a law requires pedestrians crossing a highway at night to wear taillights.

hit the road when you willingly go on a blind date with your parent's friend's son.

Arms and Dangerous:

Best for passengers. If you're sitting on the right side of the car, grasp the handle of the window crank in your right hand and roll the window up and down as fast as you can. Then switch hands without changing positions in the car. Be sure to work out both arms when sitting on the right side as well as on the left side. If your car has automatic windows, you're probably spoiled and lazy, and deserve flabby arms.

Recommended workout: Speed sets—work each arm for three to five miles. Aim for 10 sets per mile, but eight is decent.

Muscle group worked: Biceps, triceps, and deltoids.

Benefit: Pumps and defines upper arms—key for drive-by flirting; ventilates the car (ideal when someone has the **butt sneezes**).

butt sneezes n *loud farts, major gas, audible* **sins of emission**

sins of emission n *silent farts, major gas, inaudible butt sneezes*

> **BIG TIP** When it's so hot you feel like you're driving through hell, keep a plastic spray bottle filled with ice water in the car. A cold spritz every now and then will keep you from overheating—and it's not nearly as traumatic as ice cubes in your underwear.

> **BIG TIP** If you're so lost that you need to ask directions, do yourself a favor—ask at least two people. Some jokers just love to send out-of-towners heading in the wrong direction.

It's time to hit the road when you join a Friday night bowling league.   It's time to

safety school

When you're exploring new territory and meeting new people, anything can happen. So be aware and be prepared to think and act fast when you need to. Here's a quick review of safety tips, plus some things you may not have thought about:

Steer Clear of Big Rigs

When driving behind an 18-wheeler, leave at least 30 feet between you and the truck. If you get any closer than that, you'll be in the trucker's blind spot. After you pass a big rig, wait until both of the truck's headlights are visible in your rearview mirror before merging back into his lane.

Choose a Code Word

Every time you hit the road, you and your road sisters should decide on a code word that secretly signals danger. Ideally, it's a word that you wouldn't normally use in conversation, something like "responsibility," "chimichanga," or "catechism." For example, if the security guard is onto you, you might say, "I could sure go for a chimichanga right now." Or if some sleazeball refuses to leave your side, you could say, "Finish your drinks, it's time for catechism."

Non-gun Weapons You Already Own

Just in case you find yourself in a dangerous situation down the road, it's a good idea to take a mental inventory of what you have handy that could work as a weapon in a pinch. Things like . . .

sharp metal nail file
A quick, firm jab to the windpipe has a breathtaking effect.

breath spray
A Binaca blast in the eye stops the action in a blink.

disposable lighter and aerosol hair spray
For those hot moments when you wish you had your blowtorch along.

high-heeled shoe
A stiletto-heel puncture through his foot will stop him in his tracks.

lug wrench
The perfect tool for delivering a wrenching blow to any lug.

road when you're fantasizing about the UPS man—who may actually be a woman.

car keys
Hold them in your hand and make a fist with a few sharp points poking out between your fingers. Go for the eyes.

pen or pencil
He'll hear you say no when you jam the point into his ear canal.

gas
A well-timed release of toxic fumes is sure to clear a room.

and, of course:

your knee
Do it hard and fast with no regrets.

Cellular Phones

When planning to drive cross-country or any long distance, check with your cellular phone service provider about roaming charges and availability before you leave. It's a serious roadkill to find out your phone doesn't work when you really need it. If you're shopping for a new cell phone before a trip, do your homework. The newer digital cell phones sound clear and sharp, but many have service limited to major metro areas. If you have the choice, opt for a combination digital/analogue phone that will roll over to analogue in areas where digital service isn't available. Or just stick with your old analogue phone and use the money you save to buy more gas.

Do not use a cell phone to:

* call time
* order pizza during a high-speed lane change
* call *Car Talk* to ask why your brakes sound like mating humpback whales (callers are prearranged weeks in advance)

Do use a cell phone to:

* call 911 in an emergency (be sure to give your exact location—unlike most telephones, cell phones do not automatically tell an operator your location)
* report an accident or injured animal
* call your boss, laugh hysterically, and hang up

BIG TIP Be sure to keep the floor on the driver's side clean. If a bottle, a can, or even an apple rolls under the brake pedal and you have to hit the brakes suddenly, you're toast. If something does get stuck under the brake pedal and you have to stop, pull hard on the emergency brake.

Picking Up a Hitchhiker

It's always risky picking up a stranger on the side of the road—and sometimes it's worth it. But don't ever take the risk unless you definitely have him outnumbered. And keep the duct tape handy in case you need to hogtie him and throw him in the trunk.

Before you pick up a hitchhiker, ask yourself three questions:

1. Do I value my life?

2. Does he look like a serial killer?

3. Even if he does, would I value my life more with him in it?

If you're not sure about the answer to the last question, make a quick **Brad Pitt stop**. Hit the brakes, make a U-turn, and get a closer look. You can check him out without making any commitment. And just think of all the times a carload of cat-calling guys slowed down to check you out and then peeled off. It's payback time.

Brad Pitt stop n *an emergency pit stop to sneak a closer look at a piece of* **sweet meat** *(do not confuse with* **pulpit stop***)*

sweet meat n *a tasty male morsel*

pulpit stop n *an emergency pit stop to get a closer look at roadside religion*

BIG TIP ▶ No matter how horny you're feeling or how sexy he looks, never pick up a hitchhiker near a prison or state correctional facility.

time to hit the road when you call directory assistance for company. It's time to

Running on Empty

If you think you're about to run out of gas, slow down. Fight the urge to speed, hoping to get to the next gas station before the tank is dry. You'll get better mileage if you slow to about 55 mph (or slower if you're not on a main highway). When driving through hilly terrain, take your foot off the gas on the downhill parts, put it in neutral, and coast. Then pop it back into gear when you need to accelerate again.

BIG TIP To avoid unnecessary panic attacks, know approximately how many miles you can travel before running out of gas. And always clear your trip meter (the mini-odometer) when you fill the tank.

BIG TIP If you don't have a cup holder in your car, get one that hooks on to your window. It verges on the **minivan mentality**, but it's better than scalding your inner thighs with hot coffee. When you don't need it for a drink, use it to hold a cup filled with water and wildflowers.

minivan mentality n *the need to travel with everything—but style*

THE LAW In Alabama, it's against the law for a driver to operate a vehicle while blindfolded.

Tales from the Road

Tonight was weird. Swish and I stayed late to watch the barrel racing at a rodeo in Lewistown. By the time we got rolling, the road was virtually deserted. The corn dogs and cotton candy I sucked down at the rodeo were not sitting pretty. Our headlights flashed across a sign that said, "Next gas 36 miles." Not for this girl, I thought, as I checked the car's gas gauge. The needle was well above empty, so I flew on past the exit and the gas station. Bad decision. Down the road the car slowed and sputtered to a stop in the middle of nowhere. Swish was cool. She put her feet up on the dash, pulled out her Skoal, and packed a pinch in her cheek. We were sitting in the dark, imagining how our obits would read, when headlights appeared out of the darkness, and a car stopped just ahead of ours. It was an old woman, driving to visit friends in British Columbia. She said she was about to run out of gas and didn't want to be alone when it happened. She offered to give me a ride as far as she could, possibly to the next gas station, while Swish waited with the car. Swish was not cool with that, but it was our only hope. I got into the woman's car, and as we pulled back onto the road, I turned and was amazed to see Swish driving right behind us. We drove for almost six miles when at last we saw the lights of a gas station. The woman stopped and let me out. She said she needed to find a different gas station and then drove off into the night. Swish pumped the gas, and we tried to figure out how the car had started again and traveled that far on an empty tank. And why didn't the old woman stop for gas if she thought she was on empty? Swish said, "That was Mother Road." It was the only thing that made sense.

how to beat
the speeding rap

Crying is the best way to get the sympathy vote and get off without a ticket. No one likes to watch a perfect stranger bawling—it's uncomfortable and embarrassing. The cop will want to get away from you as fast as possible. It's a nice touch to ask the officer for a tissue or handkerchief. Be sure to blow a honker into it and return it with a grateful smile. If you can't shed tears on cue, then you had better be ready to stretch the truth—or better yet, to tell a big, hairy lie. Nothing gives you a rush like lying to a cop. And it's not even against the law!

> **BIG TIP** As long as you're not driving a commercial vehicle, radar detectors are legal everywhere in the United States, except Virginia and the District of Columbia. The laws in Virginia are very strict. Be sure to disconnect your radar detector and put it in the trunk, unless you want it to be confiscated as evidence of a violation. (In Minnesota, radar detectors are not specifically regulated, but it is illegal to hang or mount a device on the windshield.)

First Things First:

When most people get pulled over, they think it's a **butt-pucker** and assume they're automatically in for a speeding ticket. Not true. The fact is, you're only up against the one officer who locked you in with his radar gun—so it's more of a fair match than you think.

butt-pucker n *a terrifying or near-death experience ("Passing that 18-wheeler was a real butt-pucker.")*

Always be aware of what's going on around you—not only in front but also in back. When you're playing **Rush'n**

Roulette, you've got to spend as much time looking in the rearview mirror as you do staring ahead. It sounds crazy but it's true. Every few seconds, take a good look at the scene behind you.

Rush'n Roulette v *speeding when you already have two points on your driving record*

Identify Your Enemy:

If you pass a cop who has pulled over another driver, don't just whiz by thinking what a sucker he is. Get a good look at the style and color of the car and check out the shape of the headlights so you'll be able to recognize them in your rearview mirror when driving at night.

> **BIG TIP** Want to burn a cop? Buy a few nonalcoholic beers that look like the real thing, then drive past a cop, blatantly pretending to sneak a gulp or two. When he pulls you over, let him see what you're drinking and say, "We busted you, man. What a burn!" (Cops love this!) Don't do it if you have been drinking or have open containers in the car. And be sure to have your license and registration handy and your seat belt on.

Understand Your Enemy:

Forget the uniform, the badge, and the gun for a moment. Cops want what most people want: respect, control, and to be liked. They don't want to be lied to or have their intelligence insulted. Think about the type of

you can't really remember. It's time to hit the road when you pull a chair in front

person who becomes a cop, highway patrolman, or state trooper. Who would want to risk his life every day just to get a paycheck? He's either really insecure and needs a badge and gun to feel important or he has a genuine desire to do good and help other people. Either way, assume he gets a power thrill from his job.

Regardless of the personality type you're dealing with, you have to do two things: 1. treat him with respect; 2. let him feel like a really good guy for doing you a favor.

Keep the Faith:

Four things can happen after you've been pulled over: 1. You'll get a speeding ticket that shows the actual speed you were going and get hit with a nasty-ass fine. Obviously, this won't help your insurance rates and you may even lose your license; 2. You'll get a speeding ticket for a lower speed with a lower fine; 3. You'll get a ticket for a lesser offense such as no taillights or not wearing a seat belt; 4. You'll get off with just a warning. Your goal is number four. But in order to get just a warning, you have to believe that you will. And if you play your part well, you'll have an excellent chance.

> **BIG TIP** In Nevada, if you are caught speeding in a county with a population under 100,000 (most of the state), you will only be fined 25 dollars. Any such violation is not reported as a moving violation to the DMV, so it won't affect your insurance rate.

Timing Is Everything:

Whatever you say, start your conversation as soon as possible. Your window of opportunity opens when the officer struts up to your car (it slams shut when he begins writing your ticket).

of the refrigerator to eat dinner. It's time to hit the road when you called the

The first rule is to stay calm. While you wait for the officer to approach, do all the normal, polite things you would do if you were meeting anyone for the first time. Spit out your gum (or whatever else is in your mouth). Put out your cigarette. Turn off the radio. Take off your sunglasses. Check for food in your teeth. Roll down your window and wait calmly for the humiliation to begin.

Do not get out of the car. If you do, this may pose a threat to the officer, which won't put him in a very good mood. He won't know why you're out of the car and on your feet—and he won't like it.

Sit still with a smile on your face and both hands on the steering wheel where he can see them. Don't get your license or the car registration out until he asks for them. This is a form of surrender and it shortens the period of time you have to explain yourself. He can't start writing you up until he has your license in his hand. Once the officer has started to write you up, it's too late to wriggle out of it.

Lose the Attitude:

You may feel bad-ass and beautiful, but don't act that way in front of a cop. This is the time to act like a good girl—not to impress your road sisters. Just accept the fact that the officer's feelings matter and yours don't.

Once you've come up with a few possible explanations, practice them out loud to see if you sound believable. If you're traveling with other people, be sure to practice in front of them. Your impassioned performance and display of tears will go down the tubes if one of your passengers bursts into hysterical laughter.

Speeding in Good Company

You can always plead PMS, temporary insanity, or the Twinkie defense. But you'll have a better chance if you try one of these techniques developed by experienced road trippers with clean driving records. Be creative, but keep in mind that details make a story much more believable and a simple explanation is easier to believe than a wild, shaggy-dog story. And never deny that you were speeding, just claim you didn't know how fast you were going.

The Sicko Trucker

Scenario: You recently passed an 18-wheeler.

Attitude: Anger and fear bordering on hysteria.

Tears: Definitely.

Explanation: "Officer, I am so glad to see you. I was being harassed by this totally sicko truck driver who kept making lewd gestures at me." (Be specific and use your tongue and hands to demonstrate as much as possible.) "I tried to slow down and pull off, but he slowed down too. I was afraid he was going to follow me. No matter what I did, he just laughed and stayed right with me. I really thought I was in danger. So I just floored it to get away from him. I was so scared I wasn't even looking at the speedometer. Is there any way you can follow me to the next exit and make sure he's not waiting for me?"

Note: The request for help gives him an opportunity to play the hero. So it's important that you throw in a question at the end.

The Weaving Car

Scenario: There's a fair amount of traffic on the highway and you have a CB or cellular phone.

Attitude: Concerned, well-intentioned, apologetic for any inconvenience.

Tears: Not recommended.

Explanation: "Officer, thank God you're here. There's a driver up ahead who's either drunk or falling asleep at the wheel. He was weaving from one side of the lane to the other and almost hit two cars. I was trying to call for help on my CB/telephone but I haven't been able to get through. I didn't want to lose him before I could get through to the police. He's driving a tan sedan with Arizona plates. Do you think you could radio ahead to another officer who could catch that son of a bitch before he kills someone or himself?"

Note: You're not likely to be challenged over why you didn't get through to the police. Any cop knows it's hard to get a clear channel on a CB radio.

The Dragging Dog

Scenario: There's a pickup truck nearby.

Attitude: Horrified, and crazed with grief.

Tears: Absolutely.

Explanation: "Officer, I just saw the most horrible thing happen. I was driving behind this pickup with a dog tied on a leash in the bed of the truck. The driver floored it, and the dog went tumbling over the back. It was hanging there, just over the edge of the back door of the truck,

your freezer but Lean Cuisine and vodka. It's time to hit the road when you had

trying to cling to the bumper. It was just awful. I could hardly stand to watch it. I was honking and trying to get the driver's attention, but he couldn't hear me. I was trying to get even with the truck to tell him when you signaled for me to pull over. You must have seen that poor animal. Is there any way you could try to catch the truck and save that poor, poor puppy?"

Note: Don't worry if the cop does take off and tries to save the pooch. By the time he catches up to any pickup truck, it will be too late. Poor Fluffy.

The Plea to Poo

Scenario: If you haven't passed a rest stop, gas station, burger joint, or diner in the past 20 minutes.

Attitude: Embarrassed, desperate, in agony.

Tears: Not necessary.

Explanation: "Officer, this is really embarrassing for me. I know I was going pretty fast but if I don't get to a bathroom immediately, I'm going to have a serious, messy problem. I must have eaten some bad chili or something because I feel like I'm about to explode, and it won't be pretty. You know how diarrhea can be, it doesn't exactly hit at the most convenient times. If you have to give me a ticket, can you follow me to a bathroom first? Or do you think I could just go over here beside the road? You wouldn't mind would you? Do you have any toilet paper with you? I think I'm going to need a lot."

Note: No self-respecting cop will follow you to a bathroom just to give you a ticket. He has much more important things to do. Be sure to say diarrhea and to ask for toilet paper.

Speeding Solo

When there aren't other vehicles on the road around you, you still have a variety of possible explanations to get you off based purely on what's going in your car, in your life, or in your head.

The Bee

"There's a bee in my car. I hate bees! I was trying to kill it and wasn't paying attention to how fast I was going. Do you know what happens to me if I get stung by a bee? Do you? My whole body swells up and my throat closes up in seconds and I can't breathe." (This is the one time that you want to get out of the car, which is what you'd do if there were a bee in your car and you were terrified of them. Immediately start doing the spastic bee dance, ducking and dodging as if you were trying to swat it away. It helps if you have a rolled-up newspaper or T-shirt to wave around like a maniac.)

Attitude: Crazed and disoriented.

The Divorce

"No, I didn't notice how fast I was going. I was just thinking about my divorce. It's all I think about these days. Have you been through a divorce? It's awful, it's the worst. I feel hopeless. I don't know what I'm going to do, my life is going down the tubes. I found my husband in bed with one of my best friends—that bitch. Can you believe that? My best friend. I threw him out on the spot. Now my kids hate me. But what could I do? What would you do if you found your wife doing it with a friend in your bed?"

Attitude: Hopelessly despondent.

The Map

"Officer, I think I'm lost. I was trying to figure out where I am on the map, but I can't read this thing to save my life. Can you help me with this? Am I still in Arkansas or is this Kansas? I hope I wasn't speeding, I just get so flustered when I try to read a map. Do you ever have that problem? Can you help me find . . .?" (Ask for specific directions.)

Attitude: Just act like a total ditz.

The Beating

"Officer, I can't get a ticket. I just can't. If I do, my father/husband/boyfriend will . . . really punish me. He gets so angry with me. He doesn't mean to, but sometimes he just completely loses it. Once I even had to go to the hospital. I broke two ribs, these two right here. But don't get the wrong idea, he loves me a lot. It's just that he gets so angry. (You shouldn't actually say that you will be beaten if he gives you a ticket. But everything that you do say should imply that. It's a slam dunk to have a passenger jump in and say, "Hey, if you have to give someone a ticket, give it to me. I know her father/husband/boyfriend, and he goes ballistic, totally crazy when he's mad.")

Attitude: Feeble and frightened.

living dangerously

Just to be perfectly clear, neither the author of this book nor its publisher condones drunk driving. It's not safe or cool. But there may be times when you find yourself behind the wheel of a car after a couple of tall ones. If this happens and you're pulled over, it's best just to take the rap and learn the hard way. But this is a guidebook, not a sermon.

All of these methods are risky—and none is guaranteed to get you off—but they may help you avoid being arrested for driving under the influence. Most likely, you'll be arrested for a lesser offense. If you try any of these tactics, understand that you are doing so at your own risk.

> **BIG TIP** Beware. The highway patrol in many states now uses sophisticated devices called Passive Alcohol Sensors (PAS) to detect alcohol in the air surrounding a driver. They are extremely sensitive and built right into a flashlight or clipboard, so you'll never know you're being evaluated.

 In St. Louis, Missouri, it is against the law to sit on a street curb and drink beer from a bucket.

Busted!

Only try this if you are absolutely certain that you are drunk and that your blood alcohol level will prove it. Challenging a law enforcement officer is very serious business.

1. Insist on taking a blood test instead of a Breathalyzer test. This will buy you time that may save you from a D.U.I. Some states, however, have changed their laws so that anyone who refuses to take a Breathalyzer test will automatically be charged with drunk driving. So you had better know the law (and know what state you're in) if you do this.

2. Lock all the doors of the car and politely refuse to get out. This will surprise and enrage the officer, but it will buy you time. Expect to be threatened and verbally harassed. Legally, the officer cannot bash in your window or door without risking losing the case in court. He will have to track down a locksmith to open the door, which could take hours depending upon where you are, what time it is, and what day of the week it is. You'll probably be charged with resisting arrest. But after an hour or two, your blood alcohol level will decline and may even drop below the legally intoxicated level. If you're alone at night or on a desolate stretch of road, you can argue that you felt unsafe opening your car to a strange man. You're a cautious woman traveling through unfamiliar territory, you've heard stories . . .

Q: Where and when were the first parking meters installed?

A: Oklahoma City during the 1930s

the road when you floss three times a day.   It's time to hit the road when you're

3. If you've been drinking and have an open bottle of hard liquor in the car, you're already in deep shit. So what do you really have to lose? Immediately get out of the car carrying the bottle of Jack Daniels or whatever. Keep both hands in the air so the cop can see that you don't have a gun. Then, standing right in front of the patrol car in the light from the headlights, begin to guzzle the contents of the bottle. Surprise is on your side, but you must act quickly for this to work. If the officer sees you getting drunk before his very eyes, it will be difficult if not impossible for him to prove that you were drunk while operating the car. This is a ballsy move, but it hinges on the law, not logic. Your explanation: temporary insanity.

Tales from the Road

It was a hot July evening and I felt lucky. I was driving a wild, screaming carload of road-raging sisters from one watering hole to the next in an old Cadillac with the top sawed off. Naturally, we attracted quite a bit of attention. Unfortunately, we attracted a cop. He pulled us over and asked me for my license and registration. I looked at him coolly and said, "Do you know who I am, officer?" He said, "I don't care who you are. License and registration." I paused a moment for dramatic effect and then said, "Officer, don't you recognize me?" He aimed his flashlight in my face and looked me over. "No, lady," he said. "I don't. And I don't really care." "Well you should," I responded. "I am the designated driver!" He laughed, shaking his head, and flashed his light in my eyes one more time, then let us go—without even looking at my license, which had expired two weeks earlier.

BIG TIP If you are the designated driver and somehow manage to get drunk, call it a night and sleep in the car where you are.

How You Know You're Really Road Tripping

By now you should be feeling free, but are you feeling bad? Check this list to be sure.

The Bad Girl Checklist:

☐ I've "done the dog."

☐ I've worn empowering headwear.

☐ I've burned rubber.

☐ I've chewed tobacco.

☐ I've done donuts.

☐ I've used an alias.

☐ I've played strip driver.

☐ I've "jogged the dog."

☐ I've seen an art car.

☐ I've turned my car into an art car.

☐ I haven't checked my messages at home.

☐ I've called my boss, laughed into the phone, and hung up.

☐ I've lied to a cop.

☐ I feel alive.

Off the Road

3

*C*hances are your most memorable road-trip experiences will actually take place off the road. But only if you do more than eat, sleep, and pee when you pull over. Take time to explore, especially when you find yourself in a **TZT**. (If you're just going to race everywhere you go, you might as well do it at home and save on gas.) Whether you're in a big city or a spit-in-the-dust town, you have to get out there and interact with the locals if you want to pick up some **local color**. Every person you meet gives you one more opportunity to try out a whole new persona. If you don't like the reaction you get, try something different at the next stop.

TZT *(Twilight Zone Town)* n *a town that seems to exist in a time warp or parallel galaxy*

local color n *attention from a local, especially sexual ("Looks like you picked up some* local color *at the Pokey Pig Café.")*

> Sometimes the right lip color is all you need to pull your look together. Where can you find a wide selection of lip colors on the road? The popsicle section of any frozen foods section, of course. Whether you go for Warm Watermelon, Sassy Strawberry, Outrageous Orange, Chic Cherry, or Glossy Grape, you'll be turning heads for the rest of the day.

of immediate psychiatric help" category. It's time to hit the road when you finally

Be fearless and cozy up to the kinds of people you don't usually hang with. A long conversation with a **high-mileage unit** or a **hood ornament** can open you up to entirely new perspectives. Or just sit for awhile and take a good look at other people—maybe your life, your job, and your hair won't seem so bad.

high-mileage unit n *any person (male or female) who appears to have been around . . . and around and around*
hood ornament n *a jealous female, usually with big hair and big boobs, perched next to a seriously macho driver, most often seen in Corvettes, Trans Ams, and Fieros*

When you pull off the road, beware of:

Park-insane's Disease n *an illness which causes an otherwise sane person to drive around and around a parking lot trying to get the space closest to the entrance (do not confuse with* **Park 'n' Sin Disease***)*
Park 'n' Sin Disease n *1: an overpowering urge to have unprotected sex in a parked car 2: a form of temporary insanity*
The Lincoln Continental Divide n *an unfriendly attitude intended to keep a distance between you and people with money*

---

use your electric toothbrush as a vibrator. It's time to hit the road when the oper-

The Bug Splat Field Guide

At every stop, it's fun to examine the fascinating little creatures splattered on the windshield. Here's a handy guide to help you identify the most common bug splats before you wipe them off.

Mosquito
Aedes canadensis

Honeybee
Apis mellifera

Horsefly
Tabanus americanus

Soldier Fly
Hermetia illucens

Grasshopper
Melanoplus differentialis

Dragonfly
Celithemis eponina

Cicada
Tibicen resonans

Fire Ant
Solenopsis invicta

how to find fun on the run

It's simple. Start by asking around. Don't be shy, talk to anyone who will talk to you. What's new? What's happening? Where's the best bar, diner, or coffeehouse in town? What do people here do for a good time? If you don't smell too bad or look too scary, most people will be really friendly once you get to chatting. You'll never know that there's a horse being broke over at Henderson's place or a cat show at the middle school or a championship Little League game in the park if you don't ask around a bit.

Big Things to Do in a Small Town

Read local papers every chance you get. They give you a quick view of what's happening in the area and they're always entertaining, particularly the police reports. "6:15 P.M. Friday—Man reported dinner stolen from his table at Rancher's Grill. 6:36 P.M.—Sheriff recovered stolen dinner in restaurant kitchen." If you find a small-town paper you love, subscribe to it. You'll have a wacky weekly reminder of your road trip. Here are some highly recommended small-town activities:

* Test drive a tractor.
* Go to a high-school play.

* Visit someone in a retirement home.
* Get your hair cut at a barbershop.
* Get your hair styled at a beauty parlor.
* Visit the local watering hole at noon.
* Go bowling.
* Interview for a job.
* Go to church.
* Go to a 12-step meeting.
* Go to a livestock auction.
* Shop for wedding gowns.
* Attend a town meeting.
* Play bingo.
* Watch a Little League game.
* Ask a realtor to show you a few homes.
* Enter a horseshoe tournament.
* Visit a prison inmate.
* Go to an Elks Club pancake breakfast.

BIG TIP Often the best sights can't be found in any guidebook or on a map. So scan the postcard rack at every stop to learn about local hot spots—caves, meteor holes, hot springs, the world's largest rooster, and other natural wonders.

BIG TIP Send yourself postcards along your journey. Write a note about the daily highlight, address and stamp it, then put it back in the rack. Eventually, some nice person will put it in the mail and you'll get a surprise weeks or months later.

It's time to hit the road when your favorite sleeping companion is your

Wanderlust Wisdom

Perfect the art of eavesdropping. When you hear something good, it's like finding money. Here are some choice examples:

"I may be broke, but my car ain't."

"Get a good look at a man's boots and you'll know a whole lot about him in bed. If they're all spit shined and clean, he's too vain for lovin' right. If they're brand new, he's too inexperienced to bother with. If the heel's real high, odds are he's got a tiny pistol. If they're covered with mud and manure, he's gonna stink between the sheets. If they're clean, worn, and weathered, he's a man that knows how to ride all the way home."

"Why would I ever want to go to New York or San Francisco? I don't know anyone there."

"You gotta burp a lot after a real fatty meal. It gets rid of calories."

"Happiness isn't a place. It's a way of travel."

"When everything seems to be coming your way, you know you're in the wrong lane."

"Never seen her around before. Think she's a narc?"

"Driving through Bryce Canyon was so totally incredible. It was like being in one of those huge Imax theaters."

"Shirley, get a look at those girls. They're **car pooling** across America on purpose. Ain't that something?"

car pooling *v what your parents think this book is about*

dog. It's time to hit the road when your clothes and your pajamas are inter-

Small Things to Do in a Big City

With an adventurous attitude and sense of humor, you'll discover sides of a big city that you never knew existed. Read the free alternative weeklies to get the inside scoop and the schedule of events. Here are some proven big-city activities:

* Check the local paper and find an art gallery opening where you can drink lots of free wine.
* Get on a bus, grab a transfer, and ride around the city all afternoon.
* Enter a poetry slam and read your bad road haiku.
* Ask directions with a fake French accent and see how many different answers you get.
* Sing "This Land Is Your Land, This Land Is My Land" at an open-mike night.
* Join a picket line.
* Go to a multiplex theater and see how many different movies you can sneak into before getting thrown out.
* Visit the zoo and feed the animals.

* Go to a fancy hotel and crash a wedding reception.
* Find the nearest karaoke bar.
* Drive around ahead of a meter maid and feed quarters into all the expired meters.
* Get a free makeover at the cosmetics counter in a department store.
* Get a tattoo.
* Go to a police station and claim to have been abducted by aliens.
* Volunteer to be a hair model at any salon that will take you.
* Go to a bar in the financial district that serves free food at happy hour and eat up while scamming drinks from businessmen.

BIG TIP> Avoid reading big-city newspapers when road tripping. You'll see the same articles and columns that you read in your home paper and end up feeling like you haven't gotten away at all.

BIG TIP> When traveling across the U.S.A., always be on the lookout for Elvis. If you've spent any time exploring this great country, you know that the King lives on in the hearts and closets of many Americans. Once you open your heart and invite him into your life, he may appear before you. Just keep the faith and keep your eyes open—it happens.

family dinners because you're single.   It's time to hit the road when your only

the power of peeing

Peeing in the wild is a beautiful thing. If you haven't done it, then you haven't lived. When you feel the sun on your cheeks and the wind through your hair, you'll know why guys do it every chance they get. It feels good! On top of that, it's a way to be united with nature and a way to give back. And it's a damn necessary skill to have on the road, where bathrooms aren't always easy to find or easy to breathe in.

Peeing without Splashing or Flashing:

If possible, choose an absorbent target like grass, leaves, or plowed soil. Surfaces like pavement and linoleum have a high splash factor—avoid them whenever possible unless you're wearing rubber boots. If you're peeing on a slope, common sense will tell you to face downhill because it feels safer. But gravity will tell you to face uphill. Trust gravity. Your shoes will thank you.

If you've pulled over and either can't find a private place to pee or it's dark and you don't feel like going into the bushes, just open a door or two on the passenger side and make your own stall.

T.P. Alternatives

* pantyliner
* handful of leaves (check for poison oak and ivy first)
* marshmallow
* page of this book
* hamburger bun

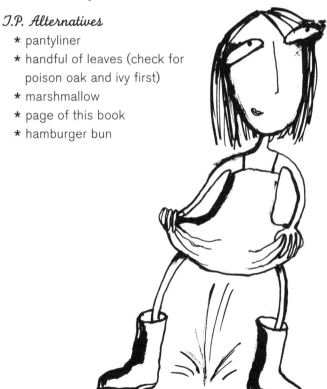

Tales from the Road

Some things you just have to learn the hard way. I was heading south on 24 with Margo, a college friend I had kidnapped from her death-by-boredom desk job in Provo. We were cruising toward Monument Valley for a little red-rock bouldering when we found our bad selves snagged in some nasty road construction traffic. Suddenly we were in danger. We both had to pee like race horses, but we were trapped, with no way to get off the road and no butt-shielding brush in sight. We waited it out as long as possible, and then I spotted an irrigation ditch about 20 yards from the road. Perfect, I thought. I put the car in park right there in the middle of traffic and we bolted for the ditch, undoing our belts as we ran. I cleared the ditch just in time. As I squatted there, enjoying the unparalleled ecstasy of pee relief and ignoring the angry sound of honking horns, I was practically knocked over by the worst stench I had ever smelled. I couldn't help wondering what Margo was up to a few yards away. I turned only to see a rotting cow carcass swarming with flies just feet away from me. Today's life lesson: look before you leak.

the joy of eating

To know a man intimately, you have to eat his favorite foods. America is the same. If you travel through a new region without sampling local cuisine, you're missing out and you're just plain stupid. In a lot of diners and road-side dives, the **scratch 'n' sniff menu** will tell you what's popular. But always ask about the local specials and the regional favorites.

scratch 'n' sniff menu n *a menu covered with a variety of food spills that give you a little sample before you order ("I could tell from the* scratch 'n' sniff menu *that the pork-chop plate was a local favorite, so I ordered two.")*

BIG TIP If you're cruising through the Southern states, be on the lookout for Krispy Kreme Doughnuts. Some people say they're the best in the world. When a warm rack of doughnuts is ready, a light goes on outside.

In some places you can't avoid **chainification**. But if you only eat at fast-food joints and chain restaurants, you'll regret it. Not only is the food generally much better at the local dives, but the people are so much more inter-esting. You may get dieting tips from a 300-pound wait-ress or dating tips from an 80-year-old hostess married and divorced five times. You may discover blue pancakes,

Secret Language of Signs

The type of sign in front a roadside restaurant says a lot about the food inside.

neon sign

Food rating:

Neon, a sign of pride and confidence, indicates a big ego in the kitchen.

plastic animal sign

Food rating:

Don't miss the chance to eat at any restaurant with an illuminated plastic animal on the roof—they're sure winners. Look for cows, roosters, and pigs. Avoid armadillos, rats, and crows.

handwritten sign (painted or felt pen)

Food rating:

Absolutely the best or the worst food you'll have. Unfortunately, you don't usually know until a few hours later. Always an adventure!

BIG TIP When choosing a roadside restaurant, look at the license plates of the cars in the parking lot. Steer clear of places where you see more out-of-state plates.

prairie oysters, or cinnamon rolls hefty enough to fill a EE-cup. You may even encounter stand-up-comedian waiters, palm-reader short-order cooks, and hair piled so high Marge Simpson would be impressed. If you get off the beaten path, you'll find a little slice of road-trip heaven at every stop.

chainification v *the dying out of independent mom-and-pop eating establishments on the byways of America due to the proliferation of chain restaurants*

How to Look Cool When Eating Alone

When traveling by yourself, sometimes you want to be alone and not have to deal with small talk or those cold stares that make you feel like a total loser. With a bit of prep work, you can give your isolation a mysterious allure while keeping people at a safe distance.

Read Something:

Don't just read a boring bestseller, a newspaper, or a travel guide. Be creative. Pick up a tip sheet from the local racetrack, a *Playgirl,* or peruse the owner's manual for your car. Better yet, read this book. Once people see the title, they will fear you and keep a respectful distance.

Take Notes:

Even if you're only making entries in your journal, do it with style. Surreptitiously survey the joint, then quickly jot down a note or two, like a detective. And be sure to conceal what you are writing, it adds intrigue. Or pretend you're a restaurant critic. Take a bite of food, savor it slowly, then make a quick note. Examine the cleanliness of a knife, then make another note. If nothing else, you may get better service.

Wear Dark Glasses:

This alone will suggest that you're famous or really hungover—and don't want to be bothered. Or you can pretend that you're with the Secret Service. Every now and then put your hand up to one ear, nod a few times, look around suspiciously at other diners, and then talk into your wristband. Works every time.

flower. It's time to hit the road when the only numbers on your speed dial are

Things to do with . . . This Book

* press big beautiful bugs and butterflies that get caught in the grille
* read behind the wheel during flat, dull stretches
* swat flies
* kindling for campfires
* blot popsicle lipstick
* use when there's no more T.P.
* impromptu hostess gift when descending on distant relatives (be sure to steal it back before you leave)
* pick beef jerky out of your teeth

restaurants that deliver. It's time to hit the road when you lock the bathroom door

Looking for Mr. Salad Bar

Fat chance of finding him on the road. Unless you're in the mood for diced iceberg lettuce and a shriveled cherry tomato sprinkled with fossilized Wonder Bread croutons, don't bother ordering a salad off the menu. The concept of mixed baby greens is still a few decades away from most roadside eateries in America. If you're craving roughage, your best bet is to find a quality steak house with a salad bar. (But check out the condition of the salad bar before you bother to sit down.) And there's always the produce department at the local grocery store. A bag of baby carrots, a cucumber, and a head of cauliflower or broccoli go a long way with a jar of ranch dressing.

Things to do with . . . A Twister Game Mat

* festive picnic tablecloth
* slit the middle, and it's a rain poncho
* works as a pup tent (with jump rope) or ground cover when unexpectedly camping
* portable changing room
* wet it, and it's a Slip-n-Slide
* play Twister—it's a cool truck stop icebreaker and a way to get physical with strangers
* windshield sun protector or interior sun shade

while going to the bathroom even though you live alone.   It's time to hit the road

Parking Lot Parties

As you travel down the long and winding road, there will be times when you'd rather have your own tailgate party outside than go inside a restaurant or bar to unwind—it could be a gorgeous sunset you don't want to miss, a herd of cowboys practicing their lassos, or a serious case of gas. Whatever the reason, just make a pit stop to load up on provisions, then pick your spot and whip out your Twister game mat. Here are a few ways to make the most of a little roadside R & R.

Cooking under the Hood

Why eat tortilla chips out of the bag with cold bean dip when you can have a platter of nachos deluxe piping hot off the engine? With a little planning and finesse, you can cook or warm delectable road snacks under the hood while you drive. Doublewrap your goodies tightly in tinfoil to keep the fumes out and the engine-fire-causing drizzle in. Then find a hot spot on the engine to set or wedge your movable feast. Just like an oven, it's better to preheat your engine before you start cooking. But be careful, or you'll get cooked.

Please note: cooking times may vary depending on your car.

Road Nachos Deluxe:

What you need:

* aluminum foil
* large, shallow aluminum baking tin
* grandé bag of tortilla chips
* can of bean dip
* package of shredded cheddar cheese
* sliced chili peppers

What to do:

Spread the bean dip on the bottom of the tin, pour the chips over the bean dip, add chili peppers according to taste, then sprinkle with shredded cheese. Seal top with aluminum foil. Secure baking tin in place. Cook for 45 minutes at 60 mph or 60 minutes at 40 mph. Serves two road sisters and one hitchhiker.

Frito Pie:

What you need:

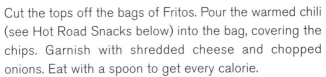

* small bags of Fritos corn chips
* large can of chili
* package of shredded cheese
* chopped onions

What to do:

Cut the tops off the bags of Fritos. Pour the warmed chili (see Hot Road Snacks below) into the bag, covering the chips. Garnish with shredded cheese and chopped onions. Eat with a spoon to get every calorie.

Hot Road Snacks	Cooking Instructions
cinnamon rolls	20 minutes at 60 mph
pizza (if frozen)	75 minutes at 65 mph
hot dogs	30 minutes at 55 mph
mini quiche (if frozen)	60 minutes at 65 mph
chili	40 minutes at 55 mph
s'mores	30 minutes at 55 mph
fillet of sole (add butter, salt, pepper, lemon juice, and sprinkle with parsley)	50 minutes at 65 mph

when your running shoes look brand new and they're two years old. It's time to

14 Ways to Open a SODA

If you're caught roadside without a bottle opener, no problem.

Every car has so many easy ways to open a beer bottle, it's hard to understand why they don't teach this in driver's ed. The techniques that work best are the traditional **Wedge-and-Push** and the **Hook-and-Pop**, for more desperate situations. To Wedge-and-Push, hook the edge of the bottle cap between two hard surfaces, then push down gently. To Hook-and-Pop, hook the back edge of the bottle cap on a strong metal edge, then pop the bottle top hard with the heel of your hand. (Avoid using any part of the car that's made of plastic or flimsy metal.)

Here are 14 potential bottle openers:

1. **U-shaped ring where the front doors latch.** Just open the car door, find the ring on the side of the car, and Wedge-and-Push.

2. **Hubcap.** Either technique can work. Try to use a horizontal opening so you won't spill a drop.

3. **Rear window windshield wiper.** Wedge the bottle top under the wiper arm and against the back of the car. Use a rag to help it hold and to avoid scratching the paint.

4. **Armrests on the driver's or passenger's door.** Just wedge it in the space between the door and the armrest and push down.

5. **Front grille.** Either technique can work, but be careful. Some grilles look like metal, but they're actually plastic.

6. **Rain gutter.** Trucks and S.U.V.'s have the widest gutters. Your best bet is right next to the front windshield, where the angle minimizes spillage.

7. **Underneath the hood.** Open the hood and look up for any opening between the two layers of metal where you can wedge a bottle in, then pull.

8. **Underneath the trunk.** Same as underneath the hood.

9. **License plate.** Works best without a license-plate holder. Just hook the bottle cap on the top edge and pop it down good and hard.

10. **Luggage rack.** Every one is different, so just explore.

11. **Door hinges.** Open the door as wide as possible. Depending upon your car, you can probably find a way.

12. **Side-door ashtrays.** Remove the whole ashtray, then wedge the bottle top into the empty space, hook the bottle cap on the upper lip, and push down.

13. **Metal bumper.** Make sure it's metal, then find a solid edge, and just Hook-and-Pop.

14. **Tow ring.** All cars have a tow ring underneath the front bumper. Most are perfect for a quick Wedge-and-Push.

the truck stop–
America's Beautiful Oasis

Authentic big-ass truck stops are a world of their own. They are a traveler's oasis where you can find virtually anything you need—good eats, a fax machine and copier, an ATM, a cheap shower, unusual conversation, plus anything from a sleazy novel or a lug wrench to a chocolate-flavored condom or a new outfit. If you pick up a pair of LongHaul jeans, you'll be traveling in style (no nasty crotch grip!) and could set a trend back home.

 Some truck stops rent books on tape that you can take with you and drop at a truck stop two or three states away.

The Princess Phone

When you see a princess phone, you know you're in **Big Hair Country**. You'll find many delights in a truck-stop restaurant—breakfast 24 hours a day, huge servings, fair prices, free breath mints, and a princess phone on every table or even along the counter. There's something sweet about seeing a big, burly guy chatting away with his honey on a dainty little princess phone while he shovels down a plateful of hash. These phones are there to be used. So don't be shy, whip out your calling card and dial up a storm. Remember, if you're calling an authority figure or unfriendly party to gloat, don't stay on the line for more than 30 seconds or your call can be traced.

Big Hair Country n *hair as wide as a state, as long as a mall, or tall enough to block your view of a sunset (you'll know it when you see it)*

Trucker Chic

The trucker's uniform has a distinct style. It signifies a man's profession, his pride, and tells you where he calls home. Trucker chic is a perfect balance of function and fashion. Every item, even the accessories, are designed to be comfortable, to serve a purpose, and to communicate.

You start with the boots. They can be cowboy boots, logger boots, or work boots—but they must be big, kick-some-ass boots. (No real trucker would be caught dead in sneakers!)

Then you've got the jeans, always jeans. Usually it's Wrangler or Lee, maybe LongHaul or Levi's—but never anything flashy or anything without a label.

Shirts are worn layered for quick climate control, a T-shirt underneath and a woven shirt on top.

Accessories are key. The hat is a must. If it's a baseball cap, it not only hides oily hair, it's also a tiny billboard that acts as a calling card. It might say "Peterbilt," "Skoal," "UT," or "Big Daddy," but you know it means something and you had better pay attention. If it's a cowboy hat, enough said.

The belt buckle is the badge of honor—usually worn over to the side so it won't cut into their beer belly when they're behind the wheel. The bigger the buckle, the bigger the man. Don't be afraid if you see a belt buckle the size of a small dinner plate, just tip your hat and move on.

> **BIG TIP** Bad girls are always big tippers. It's a sister thing. Leave a couple of extra bucks plus a souvenir, a fortune, or a short note with a pearl of wisdom you've learned on your journey. If you share the wealth of your freedom, it's good for your soul and good for your car-ma.

the necessity of sleeping

The rush of the road can make you feel invincible. But even a bad girl needs to sleep some time. So find a road-side motel before you hit E for exhaustion—it's much more fun to crash on a bed than into a tree. One of the sweetest treats of road tripping is the simple fact that for about 25 bucks a night, you can sleep somewhere safe and never, ever have to pick up after yourself or anyone else. No phone calls to answer, no dishes to do, no bills to pay, no messes to clean up, no one to take care of—no worries. But the best part of touring the cheap motel circuit is being able to take a hot bath every night without ever cleaning tub scum. If there is a little mold in the tile, just bathe wearing sunglasses—you won't see a thing you can't handle.

Getting the Best Rate

Always ask the rate before taking a room—and never accept the first price you're quoted. Unless it's peak season or there's a rodeo or festival in town, you can easily negotiate down. But you do this because you can, not because you need to, regardless of your budget. Go to a few different motels (they tend to grow in clusters beside the road) and do some competitive shopping. If no one is budging, eat dinner and try again two hours later. Be sure to ask about perks and bennies: coffee in the room, free shampoo and conditioner, Magic Fingers vibrating beds, continental breakfast. All these things can be deal makers or breakers. Make sure they know it.

Places to Sleep in Your Car

Good	Bad
* a residential neighborhood	* near a bar
* any truck stop parking lot	* a school parking lot
* a cemetery	* a deserted rest stop
* a motel parking lot	* private property
* right next to a used-car lot	
* near a 24-hour shopping mall	

Negotiating Tips:

When a motel manager quotes you a price, wince and look away. Then dig through your purse or backpack for your wallet. Look inside your wallet, shake your head, and wince again, then sheepishly ask, "Do you have anything cheaper?" A well-timed wince goes a long way. And don't forget to ask about discount group rates. "Do you have room discounts for members of AAA, AA, or the NRA? Are you sure?"

Five things to keep in mind:

1. You don't have to pay the advertised room rate—that's for suckers.

2. The further you drive from the exit, the cheaper the rate.

3. The later it is, the better your chances of negotiating down.

4. Motel owners would rather get something for a room than have it sit empty overnight.

5. Pushy bitches don't get better rates.

Creative Payment:

If you're really desperate or broke, you can always try to barter. Fortunately, once you escape the big cities, you'll find the barter system still thrives in America. Be shameless, be charming, be creative. A little charisma goes a long way.

In exchange for a room, offer to . . .

perform in the hotel lounge

Do you juggle, sing, dance, play the accordion, or remember your pompom routine from high school? That ought to do it.

plug their motel in the article you're writing on crossing America

Ask some questions, take a few notes, gather any brochures, and frequently start sentences with, "My damn editor is so demanding . . ."

change sheets, do dishes, paint rooms, mop floors

If you're pathetic enough, they'll probably feel sorry for you and cut you a break.

bake your famous cinnamon sticky buns for the breakfast buffet

When you get to the room, call your mom and beg for a recipe.

road when you're beginning to think that being a teenager wasn't so bad. It's

Tales from the Road

Last night we tried to make it to South Bend to find a cheap motel, but we missed a turn someplace. By the time we figured that out, it was after midnight and we were too tired to go back, so we decided to pull off the road and just sleep in the car. We drove a few miles from the main road looking for a safe spot and found a quiet little lane. I killed the lights so we wouldn't attract unwanted attention. We couldn't see a thing as we inched along. Finally I thought I saw a big tree over on the left and pulled the car toward it out into an open field. We had been telling ghost stories all evening and were afraid to explore in the dark, so we just peed a few yards from the car, then reclined the front seats, got into our sleeping bags, and went to sleep. Around dawn the sound of rain woke me. I poked my head up and saw a man holding a spraying garden hose in one hand and a shotgun in the other. A few yards behind the man was the back porch of his house. We had spent the night parked on his back lawn. After I explained the situation and apologized about 10 times, his wife was kind enough to invite us in for breakfast. They even let us use their bathroom.

car troubleshooting

The Damn Thing Won't Start

If you've left your lights on over night or the radio on while **auto-mating** deep into the night, your battery is probably dead.

auto-mating v *having sex in a car*

Jump-Start:

What you'll need:

* jumper cables
* a solid citizen with a healthy car and battery who's willing to lend a hand, or a fast-talking hustler who'll swap a hubcap for a jump.

What to do:

1. Locate your solid citizen or slick hustler using the universal hand sign for "I need a jump." Stand with both arms extended above your head and pinch your fingers open and closed like a lobster. (Anyone who doesn't know this sign will most likely stop and direct you to the nearest mental hospital.)

2. Put both cars in park or neutral, set the emergency brakes, and turn off the car.

3. Take off the caps from both batteries.

4. Red=Positive, Black=Negative

Attach one of the red clips to the positive terminal of your battery (the positive terminal will be marked by "+"

or "pos" or it will be bigger than the negative) and the other end to your new best friend's battery. Now attach one of the black clips to the negative terminal of the other car and the other end to a metal (not aluminum) surface near the carburetor or battery.

BIG TIP Jumping a start isn't as dangerous as you might think. Don't worry about a few sparks—this is normal. But, unless you want an instant perm, do not:

* touch the metal clips
* touch the metal clips together
* lean on the car with one hand while attaching a clip to the battery with the other hand.

5. Get into your car and start it. If it doesn't start, check the cable connections and try again. If it still won't start, run the other car with the cables still connected for about five minutes and then try again. Once your car has started, keep the engine running for 10 to 15 minutes to allow your battery to recharge. Don't turn off the ignition right away or your battery will still be dead.

Push-Start:

For cars with manual transmission, the old push-start technique is worth a try.

What you need:

* a couple of people who can push a car, or a decent-size hill
* a little luck

What to do:

Put the car in neutral and release the emergency brake. With one person behind the wheel, give the car a good running push. Once the car has a little momentum, say a few Hail Marys, put the car in first gear, pop the clutch, and give it some gas. Hopefully the car will miraculously start.

Push starting also can be done solo (it helps if you just happen to be at the top of a hill). With the driver's side door open, give the car a big heave-ho, get it going as fast as you can, then take a running leap into the front seat. Anything's possible.

you realize you're still living with your parents. It's time to hit the road when your

Tow Time:

If you still can't get it started, you'll need a tow to the nearest gas station. Now, you can wait hours for a tow truck or get the immediate satisfaction of a do-it-yourself tow job (and save some bucks). Like most do-it-yourself projects, there's always a small risk involved—but that's half the fun.

What you need:

* a Good Samaritan to drive the lead car
* a jump rope or duct tape and a pair of old panty hose (support hose work best)

What to do:

Using a jump rope, tie the two bumpers together (leave a few inches for clearance during turns, but not so much that your cars will be damaged if they smash bumpers). If either car has newer bumpers that connect to the body, then look for a tow ring underneath the dead car and look inside the trunk of the live car for a place to loop the jump rope.

Using panty hose and duct tape, tie a knot in the legs right at the crotch, then wrap the crotch around the bumper so one leg is above it and the other below it. Now tightly braid or twist the two legs until you have about six inches of stocking left and tie the stocking feet around the other bumper. (Slip knots are not recommended.) Then wrap the duct tape around one bumper, wind it tightly around the entire length of stocking, and wrap it around the other bumper. Drive slowly and pray for a close gas station.

BIG TIP If your car dies and cannot be resuscitated, just call 1-800-421-7253 to find the nearest Rent-A-Wreck. Your car may stop running, but you don't have to.

boyfriend thinks everything is about him. It's time to hit the road when you're

Things to do with . . . A Jump Rope

* tie rude passengers or garage-sale finds to the luggage rack
* a quick roadside workout to wake you up when you're falling asleep at the wheel
* use as a clothesline between two chairs at a motel, two trees, or two road sisters
* emergency dog leash
* tie two bumpers together to tow a car
* hog-tie impolite hitchhikers
* a belt for semiformal occasions
* divide up territories inside the car during feuds

excited to go to the dentist because it means you only have to work a half-day.

Common Gas Station Rip-offs

If your car is having serious trouble on the road and you aren't an expert mechanic, you're at the mercy of a greasy stranger you probably shouldn't trust. But there are many ways to reduce your chances of being ripped off. First, be very specific about your car's problem—it smells like a rotten egg, or it sounds like a low-flying helicopter, or it only happens when I laugh. Ask a lot of questions about the nature of the problem and always demand a detailed estimate in writing before authorizing any work on your car.

Diagnostic Test Rip-offs:

Don't agree to a general diagnostic test or a scope test (about 60 dollars) when there's a test specific to the problem. If you don't know, ask. For example, if your car won't start, it's probably a bad alternator. So ask for a charging system test (about 20 dollars), which will immediately verify the problem.

Preventive Maintenance Rip-offs:

If a mechanic recommends preventive maintenance that's unrelated to the immediate problem, don't do it. (Things like flushing out the cooling system or changing the transmission oil.) Every car has a different maintenance schedule—he won't know the schedule for your car off the top of his head. If you're unsure, check your owner's manual to see whether or not it's really necessary based upon your car's mileage. Newer cars do not need to be serviced nearly as often as older cars, but a lot of mechanics pretend not to know this.

It's time to hit the road when you have to get your car out of city limits or risk

Parts Rip-offs:

These days most repair estimates are computer-generated, and the price for the part you need will be for a high-priced name-brand part. What you get, however, will probably be a cheapo generic part. Unfortunately, you'll be charged for the high-priced part. Always ask for the old part that needed replacing to be returned to you in the box that the new part came in. If the box looks generic, then so is the part you got. If you suspect that you got a cheapo part, demand the cheapo price that it's worth. (Generic parts cost about 30 percent less than name-brand parts.) If he hassles you, threaten to report him to the Better Business Bureau or set his garage on fire.

Labor Rip-offs:

Just like the estimate for parts, a computer will kick out an individual labor charge for each repair on the estimate, even though the repairs are being done at the same time. Look carefully at the estimate for labor, if you see doubling up, call him on it. Your best bet is to stay in the garage while the work is being done and watch. Check the time he starts your work and when he finishes, deducting for coffee breaks, bathroom breaks, and phone calls. You don't have to offer to pass him the wrenches, but the more involved you are in the repair, the less likely you are to get scammed.

Q: The Interstate Highway System originally included over 41,000 miles of toll-free superhighways. What year was it inaugurated?
A: 1956

being booted due to unpaid parking tickets.   It's time to hit the road when even

Gas Charge Rip-offs

When buying gas with a credit card, be sure that the amount you're charged matches the amount on the pump. Enterprising gas station attendants have been known to add a five-dollar tip for their services to the total amount. If you don't say anything, they simply pocket the extra charge.

> **BIG TIP** If you pull into a small town and know you have an engine problem that will require parts and labor, do a little advance work before you hit the gas station. Stop at a nearby store, diner, or bar and have a chat with the owner, a hostess, or a bartender. Get a recommendation for a mechanic and the name of the person you chat with. Then when you talk to the mechanic, you can say, "I'm visiting my Aunt Penny, my godmother Fay Ellen, my Granddaddy Walter, and she/he said you were the best in town." You'll be less likely to get ripped off if the mechanic thinks you're related to a local.

> **BIG TIP** If you have car trouble in a big city, try to find a dealer for your model car. At least you'll know you won't be ripped off any more than usual.

the cat looks at you like you're letting him down. It's time to hit the road when

Coffee Brake!

A cup of good, strong coffee is mother's milk, a buzz saw through the brain, and a reason to live until cocktail hour. Tragically, it's hard to find a decent cup of joe in most diners. You've probably tasted saliva with more kick than most of the brown water passed off as coffee.

In moments of complete caffeine deprivation, it's time for . . .

Road Brew

You can pick up everything you need to brew killer coffee in a pit stop at a grocery store or convenience mart. What you need:

* a knee-high stocking (preferably clean)
* a bottle of flat mineral water
* a vacuum-packed individual package of gourmet ground coffee (about one-third of a cup)

What to do:

Take a few big swigs of water from the bottle, then stuff the foot of the stocking inside, leaving a couple of inches sticking out the top. Pour the entire contents of the ground coffee into the stocking and let it trickle into the bottle. Screw the bottle cap on tight so that it holds the top of the stocking in place. Turn the bottle on its side, then leave it in the sun. In about 30 minutes, you'll have a bottle of depth-charge road brew. (The longer you let it steep, the stronger the brew.) Then just pull in to a 7-Eleven to heat up a few cups in a microwave or drink it cold over ice.

 BIG TIP For a buzz that'll curl your nose hairs, make road brew with caffeinated water like Aqua Java or Water Joe.

the cheapest flight out of town costs more than you have in your savings account.

clean is a state of mind

Bad Girl Showers

When you're on a budget or on the lam, you can't always shower in the privacy of your own motel bathroom. Fortunately, there are plenty of ways to get a free or cheap shower without sleeping with a stranger.

The Girls Locker Room:

Amazingly enough, high-school locker rooms are almost always open during the day. This is a good bet during the summer, when lots of unfamiliar people are going in and out. If you try this during the school year, you're less likely to get busted if you go in the afternoon. But if someone does ask to see your student ID, just explain that you are the new assistant tennis/volleyball/track coach and that there's no hot water at home. Then smile and move fast.

The Health Club:

If you're passing a good-size town, flip through the local yellow pages and find the nearest big-name health club. (And write down the names and addresses of a few others.) Then put on whatever you have that most resembles workout wear and drop by the club of your choice. Here's all you have to say: "Hi, I'm thinking of joining a health club. But before I make my decision, I want to

It's time to hit the road when you get back to your desk to find that your voice mail

check out a few. Do you have a free day pass for me?"

Piece of cake. If they ask what other clubs you are considering, just whip out your list. You may have to endure a sales pitch. But after a long workout, steam, sauna, and shower, you'll have forgotten all about it.

The Truck Stop:

Most major truck stops have clean, private shower facilities. For a few bucks, you can clean up real good and meet some very nice gentlemen. Some truck stops even offer a free shower with any purchase. Just ask at the front.

The No-Tell Motel:

You'd be surprised by the number of motel guests who leave the door unlocked or ajar when checking out. In a time of need, an open door is an open invitation to a free, hot shower. One quick check for the maid and you're in. It's safe to assume that you have 10 to 20 minutes before anyone from housekeeping shows up. You'll probably find a clean towel inside. But just in case, you may want to borrow a couple of towels off the maid's cart in advance and grab a bar of soap while you're at it. If a maid does walk in on you, just yell, "Had to use the bath-

is full. It's time to hit the road when your Mr. Potato Head toy has been wearing

room one more time. Out in 10 minutes!" She'll be much more interested in moving on to the next room than getting any more information from you.

And remember, checkout time is usually 11:00 A.M.

The Fun-in-the-Sun Shower:

In the morning, fill one or two large Ziploc bags with water. Put something dark or reflective down on the sundeck (the area beneath the rear window) and set the bags on top where they can get direct sun. By mid-afternoon, the water should be the perfect temperature for an outdoor shower. Wrap a little duct tape around the bag and hang it from a tree branch or stop sign. Then poke a few holes in the bag and scrub like crazy. You can also try this with a gallon jug of water.

Disposable Diaper Sponge Bath:

If you smell so ripe you're attracting flies, but you can't swing a real shower, pick up some Huggies or Pampers. Wet one down and give yourself a quick sponge bath. You'll be smelling baby-fresh for hours.

The Do-It-Yourself Car Wash:

For a few quarters you can enjoy a public shower and wash your car. Unless you want to make a lot of friends real fast, shower in a bathing suit. And, if possible, bring your own shampoo and body gel. Their soap will get you clean but it also may eat away a few layers of skin and give you a Turtle Wax finish. The good news: managers are rarely on-site, so you can shower as long as you want. The bad news: the water's usually ice-cold.

The Laundry Quandary

If your clothes are so disgusting that you're being refused service, even at truck stops, you may be forced to do a little laundry on the road. When it's hot enough, you can just do a **wash 'n' wear**. If you're not into the drip-dry look or it's just too cold, have a laundromat toga party. Strip the sheets off the motel beds, preferably after you've slept in them, pile your dirty clothes in a heap, and wrap yourself in a toga. Then visit the local laundromat wearing nothing but your toga and turn it into a party. Be sure to make it back to the room before checkout time so you can change into your clean clothes and go.

wash 'n' wear v *showering in your clothes, scrubbing them with bath soap or shampoo, and hitting the road (ideal for convertible driving in the heat of the summer)*

a couple friends can easily polish off three bottles of wine at dinner (even on a

off-road emergency body work

The next time you pull over, crank the tunes and try a few of these exercises to get your motor running. They're real crowd-pleasers at truck stops, rest stops, and stoplights.

Hood Presses:

Unlatch the hood and kneel on the ground facing the car. (You may want to take off your shoes and use them to cushion your knees.) Or sit on the bumper and face away from the car. Raise and lower the hood in slow repetition. If the weight of the hood isn't enough for you, then tie a gallon of water to the hood ornament. If that doesn't do it, get a lightweight to "hood surf." Best done to loud music.

Recommended workout: Three sets of 30 or until the hood surfer wipes out.

Muscle group worked: Deltoids, lats, and biceps.

Benefit: Works shoulders and back; cools the engine.

Jackin' Jill:

Make sure that the emergency brake is on and that no one is in the car. Place the jack underneath the car as if you were going to change a flat tire. If you have any question about where to position the jack, refer to tire-changing instructions (page 80). Pump the jack handle in a smooth, steady rhythm until you reach the top, then lower. Repeat. Don't do this on a slope unless you want to become eligible for handicapped parking.

Recommended workout: Three sets of four or until someone pulls over to see if you need help.

Muscle group worked: Biceps, triceps, and deltoids.

Benefit: Serious upper body workout; an excellent way to meet local Good Samaritans.

Slam and Jam:

More fun with a partner, but can be done alone. Each person stands on either side of the car with the doors open. At an agreed-upon moment, both jammers slam their doors and take off running counterclockwise around the car. Each time you get to a car door, you have to open it all the way and slam it shut. Yes, it's a race, and the person who catches up to the other one wins. Works for two-door and four-door models. With a hatchback, three can play.

Recommended workout: If it's a fair match, best of three.

Muscle group worked: All.

Benefit: More fun than a barrel of monkeys; a highly effective way to relieve tension and resolve passenger feuds.

Bumper Stumpers:

Like step aerobics, without that tedious platform assembly. Stand in back of the car, facing the rear bumper. (The front will work too. But, unless you're inspired by hundreds of bug splats, you probably want to use the rear.) There are two basic Bumper Stumper moves: 1. Step with your lead foot onto the bumper, tap your trail foot on the bumper, then step down on your trail foot. Do a set of 20, then change your lead foot and

the road when you get laid off and get a fat severance package from your do another set; 2. Step onto the bumper with your lead foot, bring your trail foot onto the bumper, shift your weight and step down on your lead foot. As you become more comfortable on the bumper, feel free to personalize your workout with a kick to the side or the rear, deep squats or a back handspring. Road-trip masters do this exercise barefoot on hot asphalt.

Recommended workout: Four sets of 20 for each leg.

Muscle group worked: Quads, glutes, hamstrings, and whatever those calve muscles are called.

Benefit: Tones the thighs and buns; a novel parking lot icebreaker; good way to test your shocks.

Why Do You Think They Call 'Em Jumper Cables?:

If you've got jumper cables in your car, then you're set to do this anyplace, anytime. If not, just ask to borrow a set from a garage or gas station. They all have jumper cables and probably won't care what you do with them, as long as you return them in working order. Fold the excess cable at either end into a nifty little handle so the length is comfortable for jumping. Then conjure up a playground fantasy and jump girl, jump.

Recommended workout: 50 on both legs, and 25 on each leg. Crosses are not recommended unless you want to pick gravel out of your knees for the next 10 miles.

Muscle group worked: Biceps, deltoids, quads, and calves.

Benefit: Tones arms and legs; creates a small spectacle and perfect photo op; it's fun.

spare change?

If you find yourself down to financial fumes and you're still hundreds of miles from home, don't get your undies in a bundle. Throw your pride out the window, get bad, and get creative. Here are a few easy ways to drum up a little quick cash.

Wash Car Windows:

Borrow a bucket filled with soapy water and a couple of squeegees from a gas station and go hang out at a nearby intersection. When a car stops at the intersection, offer to wash the windshield for some change. This may not be as effective in a big city, where people do it a lot. But in a small town, it's a real head-turner and a sure-fire moneymaker, especially if you're wearing shorts and a bikini top. Park your car close, crank up the radio, and turn it into a party. In a couple of hours, you'll be loaded.

Make Condom Balloon Animals:

Dig up all those unused condoms you bought when you were feeling lucky a few states back and head to a beach, park, festival, or street fair. Blow up a few condoms and twist them into balloon animals like you used to get at birthday parties. (Colored condoms are a big plus, and it helps to wear a silly hat and tights or the zaniest outfit you can cook up.) Sell each for a quarter or put out a hat and give them away. Of course, you can sell condoms in the package directly to 10- and 12-year-old boys for a lot more than a quarter.

BIG TIP Don't keep your stash of condoms in the glove compartment if you want them to work (no matter what you intend to do with them). It's just too hot.

Hustle Pool:

Don't try this unless you're a pool shark. But if you know what you're doing, it works like a charm in big-city as well as small-town bars. Guys never expect a girl to be any good at pool, and most can't stand to think that the girl they're shooting against could be better than they are. Pick your target carefully—the bigger the ego and the drunker the better. Establish yourself as a lousy pool player, a ditz, and a bit of a lush. (Remember, this is an act.) Then bet a few bucks on a game and lose horribly. Insist on a rematch for double or nothing. If you're extremely confident, lose again. Then up the stakes once more to triple or nothing plus a round of drinks for all your friends and kick some butt. Be sure to act amazed at your luck. You really only have one chance to get it right and make a good haul.

near 100 dollars on a bathing suit. It's time to hit the road when you've been out

Play Roadside Bingo:

In many states, you'll see bingo auditoriums right alongside the road. Bingo is a game of luck. There is absolutely no skill required, so anyone in any condition can play and win. Of course, you have to pay to play (usually one to five dollars per game card.) Bingo is all about numbers. So the more road sisters who play, the better the chances that one of you will win the pot. Beware: those blue-hair bingo ladies may look blind, but they can see every little sleight-of-hand move.

Become a Performance Artist:

Put a cup out on a street corner and do what you can—sing, juggle, do an interpretive dance, recite a monologue you remember from high-school drama. Whatever you do, feel it, love it, and sell it to the crowd.

Resell Beer and Soda:

If you do a little research around town, you can find out where people hang out and target your market. Check out lakes, rivers, parks, and beaches where cold beverages are not easily available. All you do is load up a duffel bag with cold brews and sodas and cover them with some ice. Even a plastic shopping bag will do. Then go to the thirsty masses and discreetly advertise as you walk by. If you charge a premium, for delivery of course, one dollar for a soda, two or three dollars for a beer, you will double your money in a flash.

Sell Lemonade:

Hey, it worked when you were seven years old. It still works no matter how old you are. For about 10 dollars you're in business. Buy a cheap powdered lemonade mix,

a couple of jugs of water, and paper cups. Get ice from a machine at a motel or a fast-food joint. Put up a big sign and act adorable. Remember: location, location, location.

Fountain Fish:

Find a fountain or a wishing well with coins in the bottom and go for it. You'll get nasty looks, but when you're desperate, you're desperate.

 If you need a cash infusion wired to you, call 1-800-325-6000 from anywhere in the U.S. to find the nearest Western Union location.

 In Massachusetts, taxi drivers are prohibited from having sex in the front seat of the cab during their shift.

health clinic.   It's time to hit the road when you get excited about who's hosting

How You Know You're Still Road Tripping in Style

Another Bad Girl Checklist

- ☐ I've eavesdropped shamelessly.
- ☐ I've shared secrets with a stranger.
- ☐ I've had my hair styled big.
- ☐ I've peed beside the road.
- ☐ I've eaten unidentifiable regional foods.
- ☐ I've experienced a little slice of road-trip heaven.
- ☐ I've found Big Hair Country.
- ☐ I've used a princess phone.
- ☐ I've worked up a sweat in a truck-stop parking lot.
- ☐ I've cooked under the hood.
- ☐ I've slept in my car.
- ☐ I've made road brew.
- ☐ I've gotten a free shower without sleeping with a stranger.
- ☐ I've made balloon animals with condoms.
- ☐ I've never felt more alive.

The End of the Road

4

*Y*ou smell bad and you look bad, but you feel so good. Rejuvenated. Reborn. Refried. Remember that feeling. The needle on that big gas gauge in the sky is pointing to E and it's time to head home. This is not the fun part of your trip. But—like taxes—it's inevitable no matter how long you try to put it off.

The last few hours on the road will hurt, there's no way around it. You may have terrifying flashbacks of home as you anticipate what's ahead. To ease the pain, take one last trip past the drive-thru window, make a pit stop to load up on beef jerky and St. John's Wort to fight your impending depression, then have a good cry.

It's okay to cry. In fact, it's healthy to mourn the end of a raucous road trip and the loss of your freedom. Expect to go through four distinct stages as you try to cope: denial, drinking, anger, more drinking. This is normal. To fight off crippling depression during reentry, try to remind yourself that if you didn't have such a dull, pathetic, meaningless life at home, you wouldn't need to road trip. That usually works. If it doesn't, cry some more and do a little car dancing.

You can take the edge off the pain and distract your-self during the last few hours by playing "When I get home. . . ." Conjure up outrageous positive and negative fantasies of your return. The possibilities are endless. Your best fantasies will give you the courage to come home from your road trip. For example, "When I get home, my boyfriend will have done all the laundry, unloaded the dishwasher, vacuumed the apartment, and bought me a whole new wardrobe." If you're not getting a buzz, step things up a notch. For example, "When I get home, I'll inherit a million from an aunt I didn't know I had, go through my mail and find a fabulous job offer, get letters of regret and apology from every ex I've dated since I was 16 and a phone message informing me that I've been awarded a 'Genius' grant to complete my cereal-box art project." After you've completed this step and you've actually started looking forward to getting home, start imagining the worst possible scenarios. This is very important. Negative fantasies will make what you actually return to seem much better. For example, "When I get home, I'll go through my mail and find nothing but junk mail and an eviction notice, my boss has left a message saying I was laid off, and my boyfriend has left me and stolen my stereo."

When you get home, see how many elements of each fantasy have come true. You may be surprised.

time to hit the road when you start to notice your father's words coming out of

there's no place like home

Yup, there's your dirty laundry right where you left it. Something scary is growing in the fridge. Your phone message light is blinking so fast it looks like it's pissed at you. Your plants are dead. Welcome home.

Your first night back, you may need to sleep in the car to feel safe. If you have that temptation, don't fight it. And while you're there, go with your urge to pull all the dead bugs out of the grille. You can press them inside this book. When they're completely dry, shellac them and pin them to your chest like badges of honor. You've earned the right to wear them with pride.

The best medicine for easing the agony of reentry is to stay as bad at home as you were on the road. Inevitably, people will ask, "Where in the hell have you been?" Just stare them down and say something like, "Do you have any idea how long a bull screams when he's being castrated?" Or, "I've eaten live bugs off my windshield bigger than you." Or, "Until you've done the dog, you'll never understand." That'll shut them up.

 In Detroit, Michigan, it is unlawful for a couple to make love in an automobile unless the vehicle is parked on the couple's property.

your mouth. It's time to hit the road when your gay brother consistently has bet-

work still sucks
But Now You Know Why—
Everyone There Needs to Road Trip

Your first day back at work will be an ugly shock to your system. Don't be surprised if you experience bouts of nausea, shake uncontrollably, or sweat profusely. To minimize the detox symptoms the first day, come in late, take a three-hour lunch, and leave early. Do not accept new projects under any circumstances and avoid your boss or other authority figures for as long as possible.

You'll find that you have no tolerance for the absurdity of what passes for important at the office. Don't let that change. Your bad girl instincts are a healthy bullshit barometer. Your sanity depends on staying in touch with your inner wild and using what you've learned on the road. So flaunt your badness in every way you can. Develop a bad-ass office walk, a strut that says, "Don't mess with me." Wear your road clothes whenever possible and keep a round of chewing tobacco in your back pocket. Show up for an important meeting with big hair and be loud and proud. Tell road jokes around the watercooler. (What's the last thing that goes through a bug's head when it hits the windshield? Its butt. What do men and road trips have in common? They're never long enough.) Hold secret chewing tobacco tutorials in the ladies room. Change your telephone message to something really bad. Laugh at deadlines, threats, and ultimatums.

Bad Behavior at Work

Bad Phone Messages:

* "I'm sorry I'm not here for your call. I'm either out of the office or out of my mind."

* "Please leave a message and I'll get back to you when I'm done doing shots of tequila at the bar around the corner."

* "I'm sorry I can't take your call. But frankly, I can't take you either, so please don't leave me a message."

Look-Bad Beauty Tips for the Morning After:

If you called in sick (sic) from the road, it helps to look the part on your first day back. Simply don't do one thing that you normally do. Most people won't notice what's different—they'll just think you look like hell and won't question whether or not you were really sick.

* If you usually wear mascara, eyeliner, and lipstick, skip the eyeliner. You'll look tired and washed-out. No one will know exactly why, but they'll feel sorry for you.

* If you normally wear mascara and lipstick, skip the mascara. But be sure to wear a lip color so people will think you're made-up. (And, in fact, you are.)

* If you have short hair, do your usual beauty routine but don't wash your hair. It's disorienting to others—and quite effective—when you have flat, limp hair or lumpy, bumpy bedhair but the rest of you is all put together.

Fight the Badlash:

Some people at work won't understand the new you. They'll try to stifle your sense of independence and your healthy perspective on work-related crises. They may even sabotage you and your work. When dealing with these jealous losers, your best defense is offensive behavior. Adopt a take-no-prisoners, take-no-shit attitude and you'll survive in style.

badlash n *other people's jarring, often violent reactions to your newfound badness*

when you're taping *All My Children* during the day and watching it at night.

Bad Girl Pranks:

There are loads of ways to shake things up:

* spike the watercooler with vodka
* switch the decaf and the regular coffee
* reset all the speed-dial buttons on your boss's phone to the psychic network hotline, a juicy (900) sex line, and a princess phone at a truck stop in Iowa
* do donuts in your desk chair
* reroute interoffice mail to your favorite road aliases
* attach a rearview mirror to your desk or computer monitor so you can see who's sneaking up behind you
* change the signs on the bathroom doors
* set the wall clocks back an hour or remove their batteries
* if the mood is particularly tense, pull a fire alarm

It's time to hit the road when you're ecstatic about the big Olivia Newton-John

Tales from the End of the Road

I still have a powdered mini donut from a trip I took about four years ago. It's practically flat (I sat on it from Utah to Kansas). Other than that, it's perfectly preserved, which is kind of scary. If I think that work is going to be hellishly stressful, I take my mini donut with me and keep it in my pocket. It has special powers. When I hold it in my hand, instantly I'm driving across western Kansas in a topless Jeep. It's July and hotter than hell. The backs of my hands are so sunburned I've had to wrap bandannas around them. My hair is whipping across my face. Des'ree thunders from the soon-to-be-blown speakers. Life is great. I haven't a care in the world—except where I'll find my next pee and pie. My petrified mini donut almost always pulls me through. But when that's not enough, I hit the road with my laptop and fax my work in. With the help of a sympathetic coworker, I once pretended to be in my office for two weeks while I actually cruised the Pacific Northwest. I faxed work to my client, and my friend at work faxed the comments to a Kinko's in the next town on my route. Then I made the changes and faxed it back to the client. This went on for three or four states, from Kinko's to Kinko's, and the client never had a clue.

Order Disorder

During your first few days back, you may suffer from **Post-it Stress Disorder** as others attempt to impose a schedule and order on your life.

Post-it Stress Disorder n *an anxiety-induced disorder characterized by memory loss, disturbing flashbacks, and inexplicable behavior*

Watch for these symptoms: selective memory loss (forgetting how to tell time, what you did to deserve such a nice tattoo); disturbing flashbacks (making condom balloon animals and then bursting into tears); inexplicable behavior (peeing in your neighbor's front yard, jotting a short memo to a coworker on a panty liner).

How to Merge Your Car with Your Home Life

When you can't be in your car, you can bring the feel of your car inside by using auto parts as fashion accessories, party props, or interior decorating accents.

* use a hubcap to serve chips and dip at your next party
* replace your furniture with bucket seats
* make earrings out of spark plugs
* power your clock radio with a car battery
* replace your kitchen cabinet pulls with old car door handles
* hang car air fresheners in the bathroom
* attach a headrest to the back of your desk chair and hang a cup holder on the armrest
* use a car floor mat as a bath mat
* turn a seat belt into a belt
* skewer shish kebab on dipsticks.

comeback. It's time to hit the road when you're so bored you think it might be fun

* replace your doorbell with a car horn
* install a hood ornament at the foot of your bed

Virtual Road Tripping

When your scrap bucket is empty, when all of the post-cards you mailed to yourself have come home, when you've done everything else you can to keep the road thrill alive, then it's time to try some of this:

Dream Tripping:

You can inspire dreams about road tripping if you play the sound track from your road trip while you fall asleep at night.

Day Tripping:

Pop one of your favorite road cassettes into the tape player and cruise around your town, city, or county going nowhere in particular. Explore places you've never seen before or places you've passed a million times and never set foot inside.

Truck-stop Tripping:

No matter where you live in this country, you're proba-bly just a couple of hours away from a hard-core truck stop. Find it, drive there, and eat until you have to move your belt buckle to the side.

Couch Tripping:

Put on your baddest roadwear, buy a dozen donuts and a big cup of weak coffee, then curl up on the sofa and read a good road book or watch a bad road movie. (There are plenty to choose from.)

to have a baby. **It's time to hit the road when you're constantly giving people love**

Road Books

The Air Conditioned
   Nightmare
Anywhere but Here
Blue Highways
The Burial Brothers
Dharma Girl
Eat Your Way Across the
   USA
Fear and Loathing in Las
   Vegas
Flaming Iguanas
The Grapes of Wrath
The Kindness of
   Strangers
On the Road
Road Scholar
Road Trips, Head Trips
   and Other Car-Crazed
   Writings
Travels With Charley: In
   Search of America
Zen and the Art of
   Motorcycle
   Maintenance

Road Movies

American Graffiti
Biker Chicks from Hell
Boys on the Side
The Cannonball Run
The Chase
Coupe de Ville
Crossing the Bridge
Delusion
Drugstore Cowboy
Duel
Easy Rider
Fandango
Flirting with Disaster
Freeway
The Grifters
The Gumball Rally
Gun Crazy
The Hitcher
Kalifornia
A Life Less Ordinary
Leaving Normal
The Long, Long Trailer
Lost Highway
Lost in America
Love Field
Mad Love
Mad Max
Planes, Trains and
   Automobiles
Rain Man
Road Scholar
Road Warrior
Smokey and the Bandit
The Sure Thing
Thelma & Louise
To Wong Foo, Thanks for
   Everything! Julie
   Newmar
Two for the Road
Wild at Heart

The Internet

Cruising the information superhighway is no substitute for cruising the real thing. But sometimes it's the best you can do. And it's reminiscent of an all-you-can-eat roadside buffet—it's cheap, neverending, and you don't know what you're going to get. So if you're hungry for information or inspiration, check out a few of these Web sites and follow the links, or do a search for "roadside art."

www.artcars.com

www.carsandculture.com

www.eathere.com

www.edgechaos.com

www.roadsidemagazine.com

www.roadsideamerica.com

www.moon.com

www.ptpstop.com

www.teleport.com

www.truckinUSA.com

www.two-lane.com

www.webdelic.com/usacentric

route66.netvision

the call of the road

Unless you are one of the chosen bad girls, you'll eventually slip back into your old pre-road-trip ways. When this happens, pay attention. Life is not a do-over. If you find yourself eating lunch at your desk every day, reading fashion magazines seriously, waiting for some guy to call, or feeling trapped, bored, or used and abused by the world, don't get mad—get bad. Throw a few things in the car and squeal away from the curb. Mother Road is always there for you.

Drive free or die!

television show theme song gets stuck in your head and you hum it out loud while

Legendary Landmarks

Dollywood
Great Smoky Mountains, Tennessee

Empire State Building
New York, New York

Golden Gate Bridge
San Francisco, California

Hollywood
Hollywood, California

Hoover Dam
Boulder City, Nevada

Graceland
Memphis, Tennessee

Grand Canyon
Grand Canyon National Park, Arizona

Mount Rushmore
Black Hills, South Dakota

Niagara Falls
Niagara Falls, New York

Route 66
Once stretching between Chicago and Los Angeles, now some of the original road still exists in western Arizona and central Oklahoma, but most has been replaced by I-40 and I-44.

Statue of Liberty
New York Harbor, New York

you have sex. It's time to hit the road when *Waltons* reruns make you cry. It's

Divine Destinations

Area 51

The secret air base rumored to have the remains of captured aliens and UFOs.

About 100 miles north of Las Vegas, Nevada

Cadillac Ranch

Ten classic Cadillacs are half-buried in the ground, as if they fell from the sky. You can see their glorious tail ends, fins and all, protruding up into the air.

Five miles west of Amarillo, Texas

Carhenge

A Detroit-style semicircular temple inspired by the famous Stonehenge ruins.

Alliance, Nebraska

(308) 762-1520

The Cockroach Hall of Fame

Curated by a professional exterminator, this is the world's best cockroach collection because they're all big and dead.

Plano, Texas

(972) 519-0355

The Corn Palace

This local legend is a little corny but still impressive. The entire exterior of the auditorium is covered with corncobs in elaborate patterns and murals.

Mitchell, South Dakota

(800) 289-7469

The Dan Quayle Center and Museum

The only museum honoring a U.S. vice president—thank God.

Huntington, Indiana

(219) 356-6356

Elvis Is Alive Museum

From I-70, just look for the 16-foot-tall figure of Elvis in a white jumpsuit.

Wright City, Missouri

(314) 745-2349

Gatorland

"The Alligator Capital of the World," where you can watch gator wrestling and explore the swamps where alligators patiently await your arrival.

Orlando, Florida

(407) 855-5496

Holy Land

A weird folk art extravaganza constructed over a 20-year period by a devoted Christian with a lot of time on his blessed hands.

Waterbury, Connecticut

International U.F.O. Museum and Research Center

In 1947, the first alien space "disc" crashed on Mac Brazel's ranch outside of Roswell. See rare footage of a dead alien.

Roswell, New Mexico USA Earth

(505) 625-9495

The Liberace Museum

See his outrageous cars, glitzy Baldwin pianos, sequined capes, and garish jewelry. You'll be so jealous.

Las Vegas, Nevada

(702) 798-5595

Lizzie Borden's House

Charged with the gruesome double murder of her parents, a jury acquitted Lizzie and then she got a job with the postal service. Now a quaint bed and breakfast where you can stay the night—if you dare.

Fall River, Massachusetts

(508) 675-7333

though they say to use them only once a week.   It's time to hit the road when you

Mall of America

The largest self-contained shopping mall in the country.
NASA is reportedly modeling space stations after it.
Just outside of Minneapolis, Minnesota
(612) 883-8800

The Museum of Bad Art (MOBA)

Curator Scott Wilson presents a unique collection celebrating the beauty and expressionism found only in bad art.
Dedham, Massachusetts
(617) 325-8224

The Museum of Menstruation

A bloodcurdling private collection of information, devices, and ads. Only open for about five days every month.
Hyattsville, Maryland
(301) 459-4450

The Museum of Questionable Medical Devices

A bizarre and baffling collection of diagnostic devices, machines, and gizmos.
Minneapolis, Minnesota
(612) 379-4046

The Mutter Museum

See specimens of chilling and thrilling human oddities and other creepy medical stuff.
Philadelphia, Pennsylvania
(215) 563-3737

Site of the First Official Elvis Sighting

Visit Felpausch's Supermarket. Elvis was spotted at checkout stand two after his alleged death.
Vicksburg, Michigan

The Zippo/Case Visitors Center

A museum dedicated to the beauty and history of legendary Zippo lighters, the ultimate symbol of cool.
Bradford, Pennsylvania
(888) 442-1932

start painting little smiley faces and flowers on your fingernails. It's time to hit

Excellent Events

Annual Cow Chip Championship   *early September*

This local favorite features a variety of silly and smelly cow chip competitions, plus hayrides and a barbecue buffet at the Pitchfork Ranch.

Leona Valley, California

(310) 553-0106

Annual H.O.G. Rally   *June 10–12*

Every year hundreds of thousands of Harley Davidson riders from around the world gather at the Wisconsin State Fair Park. Wear your leathers.

Milwaukee, Wisconsin

(800) CLUB-HOG

Annual Tumbleweed Lighting Ceremony   *November 29*

Gather with family and friends to watch the majestic tumbleweed illuminated.

Mesa, Arizona

(602) 786-2485

Anniversary of Elvis Presley's Death   *August 16*

Join the thousands of die-hard Elvis fans who travel to Graceland every year to pay homage to the King and mourn his passing. Bring Kleenex.

Memphis, Tennessee

(901) 332-3322

Glendale Chocolate Affaire   *February 6–8*

Sample the finest chocolates from around the world and don't miss the soap-opera celebrity appearances and book-signings by renowned romance novelists.

Glendale, Arizona

(602) 930-2299

the road when your divorced mother has more dates than you do.   It's time to hit

The Great Potato Marathon   *May 2*
Runners are encouraged to go the distance carrying an
Idaho potato.
Boise, Idaho
(208) 344-5501

Idaho State Cowboy Gathering   *April 3–5*
Cowboy poetry, buckaroo tall tales, square dancing, barbecue, and the unforgettable Cowboy Gospel Singers.
Eagle, Idaho
(208) 888-9338

Liberal Pancake Race   *Shrove Tuesday*
Every year local housewives race around a 415-yard course,
each flipping a pancake from start to finish.
Liberal, Kansas
(316) 624-6427

Lizard Week and   *June 30–July 4*
World's Greatest Lizard Race
A week of lizard-loving festivities and competitions lead up
to the legendary lizard race on July 4.
Lovington, New Mexico
(505) 396-5311

Madame Lou Brunch Day   *June 20*
A bawdy celebration of madams and their working girls, featuring a parade and bed races down Main Street.
Central City, Colorado
(303) 582-5808

The Mermaid Parade   *June 26*
(first Saturday after the summer solstice)
Hundreds of men, women, children, and dogs get mer-
made-up for this annual event that celebrates the beginning
of summer. It's a bit of Mardi Gras and a lot of mermaid
performance art—and it's good, clean, tail-swishing fun.
Coney Island, Brooklyn, New York
(718) 372-5159

the road when you dress up to go to the grocery store.   It's time to hit the road

Native American *February 7–8*
Hoop Dance Championship
Bring your own Hula Hoop and watch the best hoop
dancers in North America gather to do their thing.
Mesa, Arizona
(602) 252-8840

Nudes-A-Poppin Show *3rd Sunday in July and*
3rd Sunday in August
Feast your eyes on the contestants in the world's largest
outdoor Nude Beauty Pageant, featuring men and women,
at the famous Ponderosa Sun Club.
Roselawn, Indiana
(219) 345-2268

O. Henry Pun-Off Word Championships *May 3*
It's O. Pun season for bad puns as pun-loving word wran-
glers mangle the English language.
Austin, Texas
(512) 472-1903

Return of the "Wild One" Legend *July 4–6*
Join in the huge motorcycle rally and relive the terror when
this small town was invaded by bad-ass bikers in the legendary movie.
Hollister, California
(408) 634-1100

Southwest Polka Party *February 7–9*
Polka till you puke with the best of them during this weekend celebration held annually at the Orleans Casino.
Las Vegas, Nevada
(602) 837-3627

Texas Cowboy Poetry Gathering *February 27– March 1*
It's a wild round up of real cowboys from surrounding states
who read their powerful prairie poetry and git down to finger-
pickin' music.
Alpine, Texas
(915) 837-8191

Whiggam Rattlesnake Roundup *last Saturday in January*
Roundup hundreds of live snakes and nerve-rattling souvenirs. RVs welcome.
Whiggam, Georgia
(912) 434-8700

World Shovel Racing Championships *February 6–8*
Enter this annual race down the mountain riding nothing but a waxed snow shovel, or modify your shovel into an unaerodynamic work of art.
Angel Fire, New Mexico
(800) 633-7463

The World's Largest Rattlesnake Roundup
second weekend in March
Surround yourself with hundreds of live rattlers, load up on rattlesnake souvenirs, and sample winning entries from the rattlesnake cook-off.
Sweetwater, Texas
(915) 235-5488

a marriage proposal acceptance speech in your head. It's time to hit the road

Funky Festivals

Annual Ostrich Festival *second weekend in March*
See the amazing ostrich races and much, much more.
Chandler, Arizona
(602) 963-4571

Art Car Festival Weekend *April 17–20*
This art car festival boasts an Art Car Ball, art car proces-
sions and symposiums featuring art car artists and scholars
and the spectacular Art Car Parade through downtown
Houston.
Houston, Texas
(713) 926-6368

Baxley Tree Festival *April 2–5*
An authentic little Southern festival with logging competitions, chain-saw carving, and the mouthwatering lumber-
jack show.
Baxley, Georgia
(912) 367-7731

Buzzard Day *first Sunday after March 15*
This annual festival celebrates the return of the buzzards,
symbolizing the arrival of spring.
Hinkley, Ohio
(330) 278-2066

Cowboy Poetry Festival *every January*
This popular annual festival celebrates all that is owed to
the cowboy.
Elko, Nevada
(800) 248-ELKO

The Gasparilla Pirate Festival *February 9*
A parade of ships, a mock pirate invasion that includes kid-
napping the mayor, marching bands, lavish floats, dancing,
and other debauchery.
Tampa, Florida
(813) 228-7777

when you start a Leo DiCaprio scrapbook. It's time to hit the road when you think

Lowell Celebrates Kerouac! *first full weekend in October*
Pay homage to Jack Kerouac, the original Dharma Bum and
author of *On the Road,* during a weekend of hard drinking
and free-form freeloading.
Lowell, Massachusetts
(508) 970-5000

Morton Pumpkin Festival *September 10–13*
A weekend of pumpkin pageantry, including the Punkin
Chuckin' Contest, the Pumpkin Cook-off, and the Miss
Pumpkin Beauty Pageant Parade.
Morton, Illinois
(309) 263-2491

Spitoono Festival *August 21–23*
A thoroughly redneck celebration, featuring tobacco spit-
ting and beer chugging contests, plus clogging and hubcap
stealing competitions. Hosted by the Redneck Performing
Arts Association.
Clemsen, South Carolina
(864) 654-1200

The Testicle Festival *third weekend in September*
Join thousands of other bull testicle lovers for a rowdy
weekend of sucking down over five thousand pounds of
pure prairie oysters.
Clinton, Montana
(406) 825-4868

Olestra seems like a good idea.   It's time to hit the road when you visit the Barbie

The World's Largest . . .

World's Largest Buffalo
Jamestown, North Dakota

World's Largest Cow
New Salem, North Dakota

World's Largest Frying Pan
Long Beach, Washington

World's Largest Prairie Chicken
Rothsay, Minnesota

World's Largest Six-pack of Beer (Old Style)
La Crosse, Wisconsin

World's Largest Turkey
Frazee, Minnesota

World's Largest Turtle
near Bottineau, North Dakota

Web site a couple of times a day. It's time to hit the road when you start sponge

Road Trip Highlights

Bad girls on board:

Code words used:

Aliases abused:

States visited:

Altered states visited:

painting every room in your house.   It's time to hit the road when you call

Unexpected treasures

> what
>
> when
>
> where

Unexpected pleasures:

> what
>
> when
>
> where

Auto-mated?

__yes __no __can't remember

Best reasons to lie:

Best reasons to lie down:

Highest elevation:

Highest speed:

Highest state of mind:

your house during the day and leave messages for yourself so the light will